The Art of
DISRUPTION

IMPROVISATION and
the Book of Common Prayer

PAUL FROMBERG

Seabury Books
NEW YORK

Seabury Books
19 East 34th Street
New York, NY 10016
www.churchpublishing.org
An imprint of Church Publishing Incorporated

Cover photograph by Paul Fromberg
Cover design by Jennifer Kopec, 2Pug Design
Typeset by Rose Design

Library of Congress Cataloging-in-Publication Data

Names: Fromberg, Paul, author.
Title: The art of disruption : improvisation and the Book of common prayer
   / Paul Fromberg.
Identifiers: LCCN 2020047964 (print) | LCCN 2020047965 (ebook) | ISBN
   9781640653696 (paperback) | ISBN 9781640653702 (epub)
Subjects: LCSH: Episcopal Church. Book of common prayer. | Public
   worship--Episcopal Church. | Liturgical reform.
Classification: LCC BX5945 .F76 2021 (print) | LCC BX5945 (ebook) |
DDC
   264/.03--dc23

LC record available at https://lccn.loc.gov/2020047964
LC ebook record available at https://lccn.loc.gov/2020047965

Contents

Acknowledgments

For my husband, Grant. They say you shouldn't mix politics and religion, but what do they know.

This book is based on the genius of St. Gregory of Nyssa Episcopal Church. My first visit in 1997 set me on a path of discovery and transformation that has made me the person I am today. There is simply no way that I could have written this book without the love, challenge, comradeship, and generosity of the community I am privileged to serve. The founders of St. Gregory's, Rick Fabian and Donald and Ellen Schell, continue to inspire my leadership, and I give them my thanks for the work they began more than forty years ago. Their fingerprints are on each page of this book, and I give them credit for their inspiration and love. Among the members of St. Gregory's who have also left a mark on this work are Sara Miles, Susanna Singer, Sanford Dole, Betsy Porter, Kyle Oliver, Mark Pritchard, Kerri Meyer, Jen Blecha, Mateo and Virginia Jaramillo, Olivia Kuser, Matt and Terri Lanier, Clark Cole, Dina Hondrogen, Joseph Bolling, Abby Kelly, Matthew Priest, Elizabeth Boileau, and Nick Dolce. Thank you for being in my life. Many of my friends and colleagues have also left a mark on these pages: Mark Childers, Paul Bayes, Phil Brochard, Les Carpenter, Devon Anderson, William Swing, Ben Allaway, Pittman McGehee, Charles Rotramel, Flossie and Fielding Fromberg, Phyllis Tickle, Marc Andrus, Jimmy Bartz, and Amy McCreath. You each have been an inspiration to me. Finally, my love and thanks to Grant Martin, who fills every day with joy and challenges me to become more fully human.

Thursday in the Third Week of Easter, 2020

Why This Book, and Why Now?

This is a book about the subversive work of improvisation. More to the point, it is a book about how to think about improvisation in relation to the Book of Common Prayer, the only canonically sanctioned book of worship for the Episcopal Church. Improvisation means many things, but it at least means disrupting the norm for the sake of new insight. Although people can get uncomfortable and unpleasant when it comes to disruption, there is another way of considering disruption: it is an art. One way of thinking about the art of disruption is a metaphor that I'll be using throughout this book: hacking. The artist of disruption is like a computer hacker: making something new from a common language.

People are afraid of hackers. The past decade has seen the rise of hacking as a threat to national security. Elections are lost because of hackers. Money is lost because of hackers. People's privacy is violated because of hackers. But the reputation of hackers hasn't always been so negative. In 1983, the term "hacker" was defined by the *Internet Users' Glossary* as, "a person who delights in having an intimate understanding of the internal workings of a system, computers and computer networks in particular."[1] It's the sense of delight that is the key to hacking. Instead of only fearing hackers, we can learn from the delight that they find in creating a new pathway.

Delight was the approach in which the Episcopal Church's 1979 Book of Common Prayer was conceived. The writers, a

---

1. G. Malkin, ed., "Internet Users' Glossary," Network Working Group, archived from the original on August 5, 2016, *https://web.archive.org/web/20160605204821/https:/tools.ietf.org/html/rfc1983*, accessed February 20, 2020.

group of imaginative men and women, understood that in addition to a solid grounding in the academic disciplines of liturgics, scripture, theology, and sociology, their work was informed by a sense of delight. They wanted to give the church a guide into the future that they imagined would propel the denomination into a new world.

The writers of the 1979 Book of Common Prayer were the original liturgical hackers. Although aware of the risks, they took the work of revision seriously and joyfully. They took the church's 1928 Book of Common Prayer and re-engineered it to be more flexible, more culturally attuned, and more responsive to the world that was changing around them. The 1979 text was the first truly indigenous American prayer book. Where all previous editions of the Book of Common Prayer had been imitative of the seventeenth-century English version, the 1979 text dared to break new ground in the service of God's mission in the world.

At the center of their re-engineering was the Baptismal Covenant, a pact made between the worshipping community and God that would form the way people lived their lives. This was the most radical innovation in the 1979 book. For the first time a very specific set of promises were made by the baptismal candidates, not just an ascent to the "Articles of the Christian Faith, as contained in the Apostles' Creed."[2] But the introduction of the Baptismal Covenant wasn't the only radical change in the prayer book. There were also outlines of rites and rituals that people, in different settings, could create themselves.

Chief among these is "An Order for Celebrating Holy Communion," a kind of homemade eucharistic celebration. Instead of being precisely defined as a rite, people would have to find the language that best fit their communities and contexts. There are other examples in the book that direct people away from "This is the way it's always been done" to "You're going to have to make this work yourself" in outlines for burial, marriage, and a liturgy

---

2. *The 1928 Book of Common Prayer* (New York: Oxford University Press, 1993), 276.

for the evening. In its inception, the 1979 Book of Common Prayer wanted its readers to be delighted in the work of creating the liturgy; it wanted to be hacked, to be freed for use by everyone who cared to pray liturgically. It continues to be a document that asks its users to become improvisers, following the lead of the disruptive Holy Spirit.

The writers of the prayer book seemed to understand that if the church was going to go from being a professional organization with an ordained class calling the shots to become a community of dedicated amateurs (those who act out of love), it would have to open up the operating system of worship to the people in the pews. They seemed to understand something about the future of the church that we're still coming to grips with: we have to learn to worship together in a world that doesn't share a sense of common prayer.

Improvisation is at the heart of this reality. Like any good practice, if you want to become an expert, you have to trust in the power of making new connections from older forms. Following a recipe to the letter may result in an excellent meal, but great chefs know how to take what they know about food and create something that nobody has ever imagined before. If you want to experience the fullness of life, you have to take off the training wheels. Risk is at the heart of the liturgy—just as it's at the heart of improvisation.

Maybe the most critical reason to hack the prayer book is that the Spirit is alive in the midst of the assembly and calls us to new life. This statement isn't a pietistic hope or a spiritual pipe dream; it is the promise of Jesus to his people. Whenever two or three are gathered together in his name, Jesus is right there with us. He comes to us, not as a third or fourth to our two or three; he comes in the midst of our relationships.

Whether we gather to worship with family or strangers, people we love, or those we merely tolerate, the Spirit of Jesus is there with us making all things new. The very least that this means is that we have to be ready for a surprise when we gather for worship. The most we can hope for is that we are transformed, made a new creation when we gather in the name of our Savior. In this transformation, we know ourselves once again as the Body of Christ. As John 14:12 says, we are to do the works of Jesus and greater works. When we gather for worship, using our beloved prayer book, Christ is there making peace among us, making us agents of the peace that he longs to see alive in the whole world.

The Episcopal Church is trying to understand the prayer book and how we might revise it. In the summer of 2018, the church gathered in Austin, Texas for its triennial General Convention. The question of liturgical renewal played a crucial part in the work of that gathering. Although the news media focused much of its attention on the issue of inclusive language, going so far as to report that the church wanted to "neuter" God, there was much more going on in the deliberations of the Convention.

During the eleven days of its meeting, the deputies and bishops of the church debated resolutions about the sexual harassment and abuse of women clerics in the church. We voted on resolutions about the languages of prayer and the translations of our prayer book that are used by our many members. We welcomed back into our denomination the Diocese of Cuba, which had been cast out of the church in a frenzy of anti-communist feeling in 1964. We included trans members of our Body, not as an exception but as a regular part of our shared life. Marriage rites for both same-sex and opposite-sex couples were normalized for use throughout the church. And although there is critical work yet to do, we openly addressed the original sin of racism and white supremacy in the church.

In all of these deliberations, the Episcopal Church seemed to reveal something new: we were finding ways to grow into the identity we had imagined for ourselves for decades. The Episcopal Church was acting like a denomination where, as former Presiding Bishop Edmond Browning said, "There will be no outcasts." Of course, this expression is not something to which Episcopalians have a special claim; we share it with all those who follow the one who welcomes all people into friendship and rejects no one.

The Episcopal Church is poised to make a similar claim about our worship, and the question that must be asked is simple: will we include outcasts when it comes to our liturgy? More to the point of this book, how can we include everyone in the art of disrupting the prayer book? My greatest hope is that everyone will be welcomed into this work. I worry that there will be some who are left behind.

Our desire to include everyone at the table is held in tension with the reality that the work of prayer book improvisation and disruption is too critical to put off any longer. The future began five minutes ago.

We have two tasks in this work: we must consider the whole church when we talk about our worship, and we must learn from those who are not yet a part of our denomination: those who stand outside our doors and wonder if there is a place for them inside. Time is of the essence, and we can ill afford to leave anyone behind.

The art of disruption begins with the assumption that we are not a monocultural denomination. In every corner of the church, on any Sunday of the year and all the days between them, people come together to offer their sacrifice of praise to God and to receive God's blessing of peace. Some of these gatherings are in buildings that anyone who's ever watched *Downton Abbey* would recognize as "Episcopalian." In these buildings, you will find what church websites celebrate as the best of the Anglican tradition.

But there are other places that people gather for prayer. Some of these gatherings are in prisons, or houses, or storefronts that don't look that much different from any number of evangelical churches. In these buildings you will find singing that may be unaccompanied or supported by folk instruments. Some of these gatherings include worshippers whose language of prayer is Spanish, or Gwich'in, or French, or Hatian Kreyole. In these buildings you will find Episcopalians from Ecuador or Alaska, in Paris among francophone Africans, or in our denomination's largest diocese of Haiti.

The diversity of worship styles in the Episcopal Church is one of our greatest treasures; it has the potential to form us as a denomination. And amid this great diversity, what matters the most is gathering to worship. Week by week, season by season, people come together to claim that the prayer of our many voices matters as much as the prayers of any single voice. This raises another critical question about the art of disruption: are we, as a denomination, willing not only to tolerate our great diversity, but to celebrate it?

Honoring diversity invites us to change not just our practices but the relationships we share with other Christians. Critically, it means engaging in dialogue with those who are members of different cultures. Expanding one's liturgical repertoire ought to change the community's relationship with people for whom the practice is meaningful while seeking to learn from their experience. Now is the moment to have the conversation about hacking the prayer book, disrupting the liturgy, and developing new skills as liturgical artists. People from across the Episcopal Church are not only ready to share their experiences of worship; they are already doing so.

My congregation, St. Gregory of Nyssa, has been sharing liturgical resources since we launched our very first website in 1998; at the bottom of most of these, we print these words: "Copying for local use is permitted and encouraged." This generous offering is not distinct to St. Gregory's. Many liturgists freely share their findings of worship and liturgical texts written for their local contexts. Deacons in local congregations compose and offer their prayers and intercessions for use in other congregations. Although some publish these kinds of materials in print format, the majority of resources are found online. Liturgical disruption is happening all around us all of the time.

My liturgical mentors, Rick Fabian and Donald Schell, founded St. Gregory of Nyssa Episcopal Church in 1978. In 1996, shortly after moving into our current building, the *SF Weekly* published a cover article about us entitled, "One Weird church,"[3] that drew hundreds to worship. The article covered a lot of the objects and practices that make us "weird"—tie-dyed vestments from Africa, a theology of universal salvation, and congregational dance—among other things.

But what the article overlooked, the weirdest thing about us, is that we are a community where everyone works together to make the liturgy. One of our founding principles is both a wide-open welcome to everyone and a serious expectation that, if you come through our doors, you're all in. Perhaps our most enduring value is giving work away, letting more and more people into liturgical leadership. At St. Gregory's, everyone is free to receive what our community offers. But our sincerest hope is that everyone who comes to us will join in making church happen.

In many ways, we are counter-cultural in the highly secular context of San Francisco. But our most significant counter-cultural value is entirely theological. We claim in our words and our actions that God is calling all beings into a deep, intimate, transformative relationship.

Along with our patron Gregory of Nyssa, we claim that because God has called the whole world to live in a relationship of love, every person is on a journey toward God. We make this journey following the True and Living Way, which is Christ, who is all things and in all things. Within this context, we make worship together: adults with children, believers with skeptics, professionals with amateurs.

Week after week, like so many others in Episcopal churches, we gather and make church happen. One of the most surprising things that people find after a few Sundays is that our worship is quite conservative; the basic pattern and shape vary little from week to week. When innovation does happen, it comes to us slowly, emerging from the life of the whole community.

---

3. SF Weekly Staff, "One Weird Church," *SF Weekly*, August 14, 1996, *http://www.sfweekly.com/news/one-weird-church/*, accessed June 29, 2019.

Our work is based on a shared understanding that we are all God's friends, both those of us who gather at St. Gregory's and every other human being. We repeat to anyone who will listen that God's friendship comes to us freely as God's gift of grace. And the surprise for many is that it comes with an expectation that God will transform our lives in the gift. Transformation happens in many ways, but we recognize that the experience of communal worship as one of the most powerful. Our worship is almost a rule of life: a deliberate pattern for growing in Christ. At the center of this rule of life is the commitment we each make to take responsibility for the liturgy.

People who visit St. Gregory's, sharing in the liturgy with us, often ask, "How do you get away with doing all of this?" Maybe they ask this because they believe that worship in the Episcopal Church is defined by a defined cultural understanding of "Anglicanism." Maybe they have been told that there are inflexible rules that really aren't supposed to be inflexible. We strive to express our theological grounding with delight. The liturgy is a joy for us. And everything that we do is informed by the practices, history, tradition, and texts of the Episcopal Church; that is the field upon which we make church.

But we strive to live by a rule of life that is corralled by freedom. We strive to say "yes" more than "no" when it comes to the liturgy. This is a crucial part of the art of disruption. As we recognize a set of practices, history, tradition, and texts that convene us, we also acknowledge that we must choose how we relate to these variables. If the structures of the church are like a fence that contains a field, protecting the flock from the dangers outside, we choose to walk right along the edge of the fence rather than stay in the center of the field.

We could choose otherwise; we could stay as close as possible to the safe center of the field, far from the fence and the dangers it holds at bay. But our sense of authority is that the field is broad, the fence stretches, and we can remain a part of the structure of the church while taking risks with the rules. We strive not to do this capriciously. We want to understand the rules before we bend them. Our work of disruption is more than running through the church with a pair of scissors; we want the liturgy to make us a new people.

We claim that this approach is classically Anglican, as is the art of disruption. As one of our dancing saints, Elizabeth Tudor, said it, "There is only one Christ Jesus, one faith. All else is a dispute over trifles." About a year ago, we welcomed a longtime friend of St. Gregory's for a brief visit with us. She is an academic, an expert in liturgy and history. After the service, I shared with her my understanding that our practice is in the mainstream of Anglicanism, that the structure of our liturgy is classically Anglican. After a moment, she paused and said, "I've never thought about it that way, but you're right!" A part of this genius is praying our way together toward insight. We don't begin with a perfect liturgical text and offer a sublime reiteration of it; we come to know how to pray in the practice of prayer.

The art of disruption must find its context in love. It's easy to choose some other motivation for disruption, as any number of tech billionaires can tell you. Sometimes it seems that love just isn't enough to bring the kinds of change that the church needs today. Too often, congregational leaders choose disruption for the sake of short-term goals like novelty, or irony, or a superficial sense of justice. But, as our current presiding bishop Michael Curry has said, "If it's not about love, it's not about Jesus." The most authentic prayer book hacks are those that create the liturgy out of people's experiences with love.

In the following chapters, you will read more about the practices of St. Gregory of Nyssa Episcopal Church, the stories of our members, and the theory that guides us in the art of disruption. You will also read about the ways the earth-shaking events of 2020 continue to shape the liturgy. I was finishing this book in March 2020, just as the COVID-19 pandemic began to touch our lives. Although this volume is a book about liturgy and the art of disruption, it takes an early look at liturgy in the time of the pandemic. Other liturgists, theologians, and historians will write other volumes that capture more of the findings of this era. This author writes at the very beginning of this new era in human history with humility and gratitude that nothing can separate us from the love of God that is in Christ Jesus.

CHAPTER 1

Life, Hope, and Liturgy

Claiming Hope in God's Future

What is the liturgy for? That's the fundamental question to be asked as we make the liturgy. If nothing else, the liturgy is for transformation, both individually and in the congregation as we come together in worship: our shared act of giving glory to God and being glorified by God's presence in our lives. It is the experience of worship more than the liturgical text that works transformation in our lives. The experience of glorification and transformation is enriched, empowered, and brought to life as the liturgy is related to our lived experience.

When our worship is disconnected from lived experience, it isolates us from the places where God's mission is found, neutralizing our imaginations, diminishing our hope. But if worship and life are consciously and beautifully related, hope is born anew in us. The hope that comes to life in us is the resurrection of Jesus Christ and of all the treasures found in the wake of this event. This is the mystery of faith: what we had thought was dead and gone lives again in us and between us. Hope is born in the intersection of liturgy and life, experiencing God's glory and human transformation.

Every Sunday, as I prepare to preach and preside in the liturgy, I have to return to this hope; it usually happens in the shower. Since I'm hardly every interrupted in the shower, I find it to be a place of prayer. I remember the first Sunday I placed my stake in hope. I had fumbled my way through the Sunday texts and landed on a sermon that I could just barely stand. I was beset by doubt, nagged by my sense of being inadequate to the task set before me by the church as a preacher and presider. All of the old demons of inadequacy came to me, the fear of being an imposter, the dread of being exposed as a fraud. In the midst of this shame cycle, thinking, "This sermon is crap," I was surprised by the voice of God: "I want to be known." My prayerful imagination heard God speaking the word of hope to me. I repeated the words until they became my Sunday mantra: "I want to be known."

God's desire is to be known in every moment and every place. My inadequacies and doubts are no match for God's desire. If God wants to be known, then God will be known. Despite my own best efforts at undermining my gifts and abilities as a preacher and liturgist with self-doubt, God wants to be known. Despite my preparation or lack of preparation, God wants to be known. Desire is the nature of God, and God's desire fills our work when we just show up to do it. We pay attention to the intersection of liturgy and life because it is one of the places where God desires to be known.

Our hope is rooted and grounded in the glory of God. The glory of God is found preeminently in the Word made Flesh: God's love in human form, Jesus Christ. Our hope is discovered every time we turn and see that, in Christ, the love of God is being poured out on the whole created order. Hope seems to operate in a cycle; hope breeds hope. The more we share the hope of glory, catching the vision of God's glory in the world, attending to God's glory in the liturgy, the more hope is born in us. The more hope is born in us, the more we can share in God's glory with those around us. We share this glory in the liturgy as we celebrate God's saving actions throughout our lives and history. We go forth from the liturgy seeking more signs of God's glory in the world and return to the liturgy to share that glory once more. Sometimes we miss this vision, and hope shrivels in us. But the cycle begins again.

Hope was the last thing I had in mind on Wednesday, November 9, 2016. The night before, quite unexpectedly, the political state of our nation was upended. For some, this was very good news; people of goodwill were elated that Donald J. Trump was elected president. For others, including me, equally people of goodwill, it was very bad news. My deepest fear was that Donald

Trump's violent rhetoric would result in the destruction of people I love: queer people, immigrants, people with dark skin, unhoused people, and members of my family. I didn't sleep much election night. I remember lying in bed, having an anxiety attack, not knowing what to do. I couldn't fall asleep, so I kept repeating the prayer: Holy God, Holy and Mighty, Holy Immortal One, have mercy upon us. I thought of my Sunday mantra "I want to be known," and I questioned if God could be known in what seemed like such bad news. I drifted in and out of sleep, dreading how I would talk to my congregation about the election, daring God to show me mercy.

Then, in a place between waking and dreaming, I saw myself as a little boy at my parents' house, creeping down the stairs to their bedroom. When I was little, when I'd wake up in fear or sadness, I'd go to their bedroom and leap up in the bed with them— and everything would be alright. As I got older, I didn't jump noisily into their bed—I tried as quietly as I could to sneak into their bed. The last time I thought to do this, I crept down to their bedroom and stopped just outside the door. It seemed ridiculous to me. I told myself that I was too old to keep seeking my parents' comfort, that I should be able to comfort myself. I turned around and went back to my bedroom, holding on to the cold comfort of maturity. On election night 2016, I couldn't seem to comfort myself at all. Despite my sleepless, prayerful night alone, I could find no comfort.

My husband, Grant, is a political consultant by profession; he runs campaigns for a living. Most of his work is in municipal elections, most of it in Houston, Texas, the place we lived before moving to San Francisco in 2004. On election day 2016, Grant was in Houston, working several campaigns for his clients there. His campaigns were all big wins; he worked to elect a Latino sheriff in a southern city that also had a lesbian DA and an African American Mayor. Grant has worked for this kind of social change in our hometown for more than twenty years and been wildly successful at it; he is a bright light in my life. But he wasn't with me on election night 2016; he wasn't there to talk to, to analyze election results, to help my fear go away, to remind me of the larger world and the hope to be found in struggling for justice. I guess that's why that image appeared: me as a boy, too old to climb into his parents' bed but not able to comfort himself, feeling so alone.

Finally, I looked at the clock; it was 4:00 in the morning. I got out of bed and did the morning routine, read the morning office, drank coffee, took the dog for a walk, and drove to the church. I decided that if my private prayer wasn't able to pull me back into one piece, joining others in St. Gregory's daily, sung Morning Prayer might be able to restore wholeness. Although there are usually just one or two for this weekday service, I walked into the church and saw that a dozen or more came to pray. We sat tightly together in the small apse of the church, knees touching knees, quiet weeping audible in the dimly silent church.

Our Morning Prayer service improvises on the office found in the prayer book; it is more streamlined and includes free prayer rather than suffrages and responses. If there is any one thing that distinguishes our Morning Prayer office, it is singing. Every part that can be sung is. Many times, this includes a freestyle chanting of the gospel reading. The service includes extended chanting of the psalms, always to an improvised tone taught by ear.

Sara Miles was the officiant the morning after election day. She led us in singing the four psalms appointed for the day, including Psalm 94, which says:

Lord, avenging God, avenging God, reveal yourself!
Rise up, judge of the earth, give the arrogant what they deserve.
How long, God, how long will the wicked strut around?
They bluster and boast, flaunting their devious ways.

That seemed just about right the morning after the election. I thought, "Get after those people—give them what they deserve." The hot desire for vengeance filled my gut. Yet, even as I thought of vengeance, I knew it had nothing to do with God's glory. I knew that God's desire is never about vengeance. If God is about vengeance, then there is little room for hope to be born in our lives. The glimmer of hope opened a question in me, "How am

I supposed to get beyond my hunger for vengeance to a place of peace?" As we continued to sing, the liturgy provided the answer; Psalm 94 continued: "You never desert your people, Lord, never abandon your chosen. Right and justice will return, bringing peace to the honest."

It's that persistent theme of the Hebrew Scriptures: things are bad now, but they will turn around; stick it out and see how magnificent God's glory is. And that is hard work. I pull back from the promise of God's glory, because I fear my inadequacies are greater than God; I cling to my doubts despite God's promises of love. Fear has this eclipsing quality to it, shadowing everything that glimmers around the edges of our hearts. And the most common error is trying to overcome fear through vengeance, or privilege, or the raw exercise of power. When fear takes the place of hope, I too often try to forge ahead on my own power. When I pay more attention to fear, the vision of God is more eclipsed, and I find that I do not see as God sees. I simply cannot persevere on my power alone. Then, I return to my Sunday mantra, "I want to be known." As I sink more deeply into that truth, my desperate clinging to control begins to fade, and the cycle of hope and glory returns.

Hope returned to me that morning after election day in 2016, gathered with God's beloved in a quietly dim place. The power of the liturgy began to work on me. Chanting the psalms, I began to feel the promise of God's presence, sitting next to Katherine, weeping a little, sharing the psalms with her and the rest of the group gathered for prayer. The physical act of chant, breathing together and making sound that considers each voice, began to change my vision and restore my hope in God's glory. In a dimly shining corner of my mind I thought about the ways that we would continue to nurture hope at St. Gregory's, finding new ways of serving the most vulnerable members of the community.

The liturgy insists that we return to prayer, not because it will get us on God's good side, but because prayer nurtures hope in us. The liturgy is a space where we can listen for God's voice in the reading of scripture, in the song of the church, in the intercessions we cry aloud, and in the silence too. The liturgy provides the counter-cultural experience of stillness, even if it is just for a moment. And, when we forget our hope in God's power and wisdom, the liturgy waits for us to come once more and know God. We have to return to the liturgy, to remember who we are and hear God's promise of hope to all people; in this we are transformed.

Our liturgical improvisation welcomes many different resources for our Morning Prayer service, including collects from the International Consultation on English in the Liturgy. We use prayers we have written, and we always improvise some prayer. But on that day, one of the concluding prayers was from the Book of Common Prayer:

> O God, you have made of one blood all the peoples of the earth, and sent your blessed Son to preach peace to those who are far off and to those who are near: Grant that people everywhere may seek after you and find you; bring the nations into your fold; pour out your Spirit upon all flesh; and hasten the coming of your kingdom; through Jesus Christ our Lord.[1]

God's reign of peace is for all people, those who are far off and those who are near. It is for people I agree with politically and people with whom I disagree. It is for people of every faith or no faith at all. The divisions that seem so valuable to me as a political creature are meaningless in the context of God's enfolding of all people. The outpouring of the Holy Spirit is for everyone, the fearful and the jubilant. It is in God's unconditional welcome that we find hope, hope that does more than contain fear and provide comfort. Hope in the liturgy draws us together as one Body. In the unity of this one Body, we are strengthened to go into the world in God's power, to seek and find God's glory. In the liturgy we are encouraged by God's call, so that no matter what may happen in the world around us, we may see God's glory. Our work is to heal the sick, free the imprisoned, feed the hungry, comfort

---

1. The Episcopal Church, *The Book of Common Prayer: And Administration of the Sacraments and Other Rites and Ceremonies of the Church: Together with the Psalter or Psalms of David* (New York: Church Publishing, 2007), 257.

the lonely, speak truth to power, and celebrate God's presence in creation. In good days and bad, this is the work of those who seek God's glory.

Hope and Action

Sharing signs of God's glory with others builds our hope; this too is a purpose of the liturgy. The night after election day in 2016 I spent solitary hours alone, trying to find a way to claim the hope that God promises. It was not until I showed up in the liturgy, sharing my prayer with other people, that I began to see glimmers of God's glory and a way toward hope. Although meditative solitude can strengthen us, it is the presence of other bodies with our bodies, together in prayer, that builds up the Body of Christ to which we are called. It is in the relationships we share in the liturgy that we become strong. It is our individual selves bound together in the liturgy that works to build up hope and show forth God's glory.

The next day, I called other people who are leaders in the church, and in politics, to ask them what they planned on doing next. I called Grant and my friend Dave, a political organizer and activist at the LGBTQ Center in West Hollywood. "Well, it's bad. But we have to keep doing what we've been doing. And it's going to be bad." I called Mike, the rector of a church in Southern California. "We're having a service tonight, just to give people the chance to be together in prayer." Although there were other conversations, these two showed that in the intersection of politics and religion, there were both a common challenge and promise. The challenge is the shock of a new and unexpected burden to our common life. The promise is that even in the midst of an unexpected threat, there is work to be done. Political organizing and prayer are two ways of working for the sake of God's kingdom. "Pray for the dead, and fight like hell for the living," as Mother Jones put it. The liturgy opens our eyes to see the work that God has for us in the world; the connection between life and liturgy is essential.

When it seems like there is nothing but terror on the horizon, the liturgy calls us to return to God's promise of steadfast love and faithful presence, and to act. Today, we live with the consequences of the global pandemic. It is a time when the intersection of political stasis and public health have cost uncounted lives. The world continues to be a place laced with fear and danger. And yet, we are required to use every ounce of spiritual discipline and emotional connection to say "yes" to life. We come to the liturgy to receive strength to live and act in the world that God loves. And because the liturgy always needs someone to say "Amen" to our prayers, we are required to share the liturgy with others. As we take our prayer into the streets, we are required to go with others.

We cannot risk the vulnerability of prayer without knowing that we are partners in the strange, evocative, challenging work of taking up the cross and following Jesus where he leads. I know that when we come together in the liturgy, there is power to balance all the awful stuff that may arise. I know that God's promise is true, even if it is beyond my knowing. I know that love is the key to striving for justice. I may fear my inadequacies and harbor doubt, but following Jesus in company with other disciples will always lead to the promise of God. Otherwise, all we have is that cold emptiness that visits in the middle of the night.

The day after Election Day concluded with an enacted parable of the Kingdom of God, a lesson in the discipline of hope, and the struggle to be open to God's glory. I came home a bit earlier than usual; four hours of sleep just wasn't enough to keep me going. I got home and let our dog, Frankie, out onto the back patio and thought, "I'll just lie here quietly on the bed for a few minutes." The next thing I heard was Frankie, whimpering the way he does when he feels sick. And he did what he always does when he feels sick: he crawled under the bed and threw up, just far enough under that I couldn't get to it. It was a perfect metaphor for how I had felt all day long. There is this mess that I have to face, but I can't quite reach it, and all I want to do is ignore it. But I had to do the necessary work of making things right. I had to unmake the bed and pull off the mattress and box spring.

I had to get the bed frame out of the way and scrub the mess clean. Then I had to put the whole thing back together again. It took every ounce of strength that I had to get the job done. Saying yes to hope is hard work. Seeking God's glory requires all of our attention.

In trying times, it might seem easier to stay in bed and avoid everything, including the liturgy. We might avoid the painful vulnerability of listening to other people's grief and longing. We might simply opt out of the struggle for hope. But then we are safely alone, and susceptible to despair. History promises that impossibly hard times are bound to come in our lives again, horrific messes that come down on us like a dog's vomit. There will be days when we wonder if we are going to be able to make it through. We will grieve and scream and ask, "How could this have happened?" And in those days, we can choose to come to the liturgy where the barriers that keep us from hoping in God's promise of peace can be broken. In those days, the liturgy will show us signs of God's glory and invite us to say yes to hope. Even though we may want to stay in bed, we can choose to come to the liturgy and be strengthened to scrub the mess clean.

First, We Are Broken

A few years ago, St. Gregory's celebrated Christmas with a "Paper Bag Pageant." Kerri Meyer, then our associate for youth and family ministry, borrowed the idea and prepared 250 paper bags with minimal costumes and a few props. Each bag was randomly placed under a chair in the church. We gave clear instructions not to open the bags until we gave the word. Brad was the narrator for the pageant. He stood up after the opening of the Christmas Eve liturgy, gave the word, and then it was a frenzy of paper bags being ripped open, of tinsel headbands and random pieces of fabric. Everyone put on their costume, and Brad began to tell the Christmas story, directing the various characters to move around the room as the action required. In the opening frenzy, I began to survey the congregation.

That's when I saw that Mary was being played by Betsy, a longtime member of the congregation who is more than eighty years old. And my heart broke. Seeing Betsy, a blue scarf over her head, holding the swaddled baby doll that was Jesus, was simply beautiful. Her grown son, someone I had never met, stood by the side in his tinsel halo and watched. At the end of the pageant, Betsy said to me, "I was surprised to be Mary. But I was more surprised at how protective I felt about that doll. That was my baby." And my heart broke all over again.

Before the liturgy makes us whole, the liturgy must break our hearts; it requires our vulnerability, both to God and to one another. Vulnerability is not optional if we want to tap the deepest value of the liturgy; vulnerability is where we find the greatest treasure of resilience and wisdom. Vulnerability as worship is found in the very beginning of the gospel telling of Jesus's birth: not only in the humble surroundings of the manger, or in the clumsy adoration of the shepherds, or in the craziness of a paper bag pageant, but in the bowing down of the magi and the shower of kisses they give to the homeless son of Mary.

When the magi journey to Bethlehem, the reason they give is to worship, in Greek, *proskunesai*, a compound word of "toward" and "kiss." They show up in Jerusalem, the Judean seat of power, and ask, "Where is he that is born King of the Jews? For we have seen his star in the east, and are come to worship him." The magi come to bow and to kiss the ground before the object of their devotion. Not finding him there, they travel on to Bethlehem.

Bowing and kissing are the most familiar forms of worship in the old world. In Egyptian tomb art, worshipers are represented with an outstretched hand, throwing a kiss to God. In Persia, people would fall on their knees and touch the ground with the forehead as an expression of profound reverence. In China, the emperor's subjects would undertake the ceremony of the grand kowtow, kneeling from a standing position three times. We do the same thing at St. Gregory's on Good Friday, falling down before the icon of Christ's burial, at the presider's invitation, "And now we take our farewells together, bowing to the ground in love to Jesus, who gave up his life on the Cross and was buried that the whole world might have everlasting life."

The vulnerability of the liturgy is there because worship expresses love in relationship—both our relationship to God and the relationships we share with each other. What motivates our prayer seems more about vulnerability than anything else. Whenever I bow my head in worship, I'm aware of the fact that the gesture exposes the tender place that joins my head to my body. When we bow our heads, it is the same motion that one would take before the executioner's blade. We bow our heads in the full confidence that it is not for punishment, but for being reborn in the power of God's love.

In the Good Friday liturgy at St. Gregory's, we carry the icon of Christ's burial to the altar table in the middle of the rotunda and place it near the edge of the table, close enough so people can touch it. And then we sing psalms and walk in procession to the table with flowers in our hands and lay them on the table around the image of the dead body. We kiss the icon and pay our homage to Christ, singing and processing, laying our flowers higher and higher until the icon is hardly visible any more. Then the icon is censed as the choir sings the Orthodox troparion *Noble Joseph*, which tells how Joseph of Arimathea took Jesus's body and wrapped it in a clean linen cloth. Then we prostrate ourselves three times, showing our love by lying vulnerably on the dusty floor of the rotunda, listening to another chant—"We bow down to your sufferings, O Christ"—over and over, hoping that in suffering there is salvation in the midst of all this death.

On Good Friday, we make ourselves vulnerable to death. We make ourselves vulnerable not just to the death of Christ, but to all of the deaths that are woven into the fabric of our lives. I think of my father, whose forehead I reverenced with kisses the morning I found him dead. I watch my parishioners who have lost spouses, and children, and lovers pressing their faces to the icon or the floor, remembering that all of these deaths are never the last word. This service always breaks my heart, and that is the good news, because it is only the broken-hearted who have any hope of being made whole. Vulnerability means placing our hope, courageously, in the promise of love that comes to us from God.

The early Christians referred to their weekly gatherings as love feasts. These were opportunities to gather around the God revealed as love, and to share in the kiss of peace. What matters is expressing the gesture's intention: to become vulnerable to hope by giving one another the peace of Christ. Every Sunday, the thing that matters in our gatherings is that we are vulnerable to love. What matters is that we dare to share the peace of Christ and throw our kisses to the one whose promise is to be present with us wherever we are, in every circumstance from joy to mourning. We move forward in our lives not knowing what we will discover, but the promise is certain: what we find is worthy of our love. We can show that love in the liturgy, and when we do our hope is restored.

Hope, Improvisation, and Disruption

For the power of hope to be unleashed in the liturgy, we have to pay attention to our lives: our relationships, intelligence, and experience. We must put our trust in prayer, not just wishful thinking or trying to buy God off. Hope is kindled in us as we engage each other's pain and longing, seeking signs of God's glory together. In the liturgy, we find that the Spirit of God, the Spirit of service given to us by Jesus Christ, is the companion we need in days that seem hopeless. And hope promises that we will never be alone.

Too often, though, the ways that we execute the prayer book liturgies isolate people from each other or ask people to put their trust in something less than God. Then we have to use hope as a lens through which to read the words of the prayer book and plan the liturgy with hope as a guiding theme.

For example, think about the Ash Wednesday service in the Episcopal Church's Book of Common Prayer, a service that needs to be hacked in order to unleash its full potential. The prayer book service begins abruptly; the rubric dictates a salutation and opening collect. Then it's off to a series of readings and a portion of the psalter. Instructions are given by the presider, ashes are imposed with some of the most honest words in the liturgical canon, "Remember that you are dust, and to dust you shall return." More of the psalter follows, and then the Litany of Penitence is recited, kneeling. To my ear, the litany sounds very much like a laundry list of social offences, a sort of public service announcement related to human sinfulness, unrelated to the way that many people experience themselves as sinners.

In 2014, I began to wonder how we could hack the Ash Wednesday service to resonate more deeply with people's experience. I began by looking at the gospel reading assigned for Ash Wednesday, Matthew 6:1, 6, 16–17:

> "Beware of practicing your piety before others in order to be seen by them; for then you have no reward from your Father in heaven. . . . But whenever you pray, go into your room and shut the door and pray to your Father who is in secret; and your Father who sees in secret will reward you. . . . And whenever you fast, do not look dismal, like the hypocrites, for they disfigure their faces so as to show others that they are fasting. . . . But when you fast, put oil on your head and wash your face, so that your fasting may be seen not by others but by your Father who is in secret; and your Father who sees in secret will reward you."

The reading is quite clear about what we are to do when we fast: act as if what we're doing is no big deal. But the prayer book instructs us to do exactly the opposite. Instead of clean faces, we mar them with ash. Instead of private penitence, we recite a list of generic sins that sound like a list of fraternity demerits. It's all quite jumbled and respectable.

Through the lens of hope, we can see something about the Ash Wednesday service that is easily forgotten in our socially neurotic culture: even without our penance, God forgives us. Every act of penance we take on is infused with hope, not just of God's forgiveness, but of new connection with God and all of God's beloved children. An important hack of the prayer book is to turn the penitential formula around: instead of saying, "I must be forgiven before I can do anything else," recognize that we are forgiven already, and ask, "What shall I do with my forgiveness?" The knowledge of our forgiveness is our instruction in living with others. Jesus teaches his disciples that actions in relationship matter; that the ways we choose to live with others matters.

We miss the mark if we imagine that all of the busyness of the liturgy is supposed to please God or get God on our side. On the contrary, God just loves and forgives us. There's nothing that we can do to make God love us, and there's nothing we can do to stop God from forgiving us. We can't increase our repentance in order to get God to forgive us more. God's forgiveness is unconditional, and God keeps on forgiving.

The work we have to do is to accept God's forgiveness and share God's love with others. The hard work is to believe what God has done for us is real. God's love and God's forgiveness are big interruptions in our lives. When we might be perfectly happy to walk around with ashes on our foreheads, feeling worthless and guilty and ashamed, God just isn't impressed. The interruption in our lives comes when we realize that it isn't God producing those feelings of worthlessness and guilt and shame, but we ourselves. The interruption comes when we have to ask a really hard question: why don't I just let go of it all and allow God to carry me through this life, striving to glorify God in my relationships with others?

This is where hacking the prayer book gets interesting. The liturgy makes it seem that we are more preoccupied with being forgiven than we are in forgiving. It seems like we're more interested in getting off the hook than letting other people off the hook. But we can disrupt the Ash Wednesday service in ways that get us to act like God. The promise of God is grace and mercy, to all people, all of the time. Jesus gives us the authority to forgive sins, and the gospel gives us ways to make sure we're actively forgiving. When we forgive, we're acting just as God does.

The invitation I faced in hacking the Ash Wednesday liturgy was to make the act of penance real and personal, not abstract and generic. The hack that we use at St. Gregory's is one I took from a very traditional act of penance from the Byzantine church, of monastic origin, done at Sunday vespers the evening before Great Lent begins. In essence it is an opportunity for each member of the community to greet every other member using this dialogue: The first person says, "Forgive me a sinner." The other person says, "God forgives you, forgive me a sinner." And the first person responds, "God forgives you." In many Eastern churches this takes place in a long line of people, beginning with the most senior cleric of the community seeking forgiveness from the sub-deacon. In the Orthodox tradition, the rite sometimes includes naming specific sins.

At St. Gregory's, we adapt this liturgical practice to fit our particular congregation. It takes place after Communion, as we are all standing around the altar in the rotunda of the church. The presider, usually me, says this post-communion prayer, which is also the blessing:

> O God of life, save us from the spirit of apathy, abuse, lust for power and ranting, and grant to your servants, a spirit of integrity, humility, patience and love. May we see our own faults and not judge our kindred. Blessed be God's glorious name, henceforth and forevermore.

Then we collect alms for the relief of the poor, people bringing their money to the altar and putting it in a basket. After the collection, the following introduction is made by one of the liturgical leaders:

> Just as we greeted each other at the Peace, now we conclude by sharing with each other the assurance of God's forgiveness, and sending each other out to do the work of forgiveness in the world.

The leader then gives instructions on how we will forgive each other, and the presider demonstrates. As the presider, my job is to find the youngest child in the room and kneel in front of them, offering my hands and taking theirs in mine and saying the words, "Forgive me a sinner," and we exchange words of forgiveness. Then people begin to offer forgiveness to each other. While we forgive each other, a quartet sings verses of the hymn from Forgiveness Sunday in the Orthodox Church:

> Thy grace hath shone forth, O Lord, it has shone forth and given light to our souls. Behold, now is the accepted time: behold, now is the season of repentance. Let us cast off the works of darkness and put on the armor of light, that having sailed across the great sea of the Fast, we may reach the third-day Resurrection of our Lord Jesus Christ, the Savior of our souls.

We roam around the church, asking each other's forgiveness. It is incredibly powerful. Children forgive their parents, and spouses forgive each other. I forgive people with whom I have conflict and they forgive me. Sometimes I have to stop speaking and just stare through tears at the other person. Strangers who have come to the church forgive the founders of the church. People we love and people we merely tolerate encounter each other in forgiveness, the penitent and the skeptical. All share in the act of forgiveness.

God wants to see more forgiveness in this world, and gives sinful humanity the authority to forgive. So, we need to forgive. In our homes, and in our families, we need to forgive. In our religious communities we need to forgive. We need forgiveness between nations and cultures and parties. Forgiveness is a treasure that God shares with us to see peace in the world around us, to make the world anew. We must re-create the world because God is actively tearing down the false world that our imaginations spin out of sin. God is destroying our traditions. God is tearing down what we consider to be so holy that it cannot be touched. God is putting to death the hostilities that organize our lives. God is undermining every trick we might try to win God's favor. God simply longs for us to come to full, glorious life—and to share that life with those we encounter every place in our lives.

Liturgy in the Time of COVID-19

In ten years, when we have enough space to look back on it, people will share a common story about the COVID-19 pandemic of 2020: "I remember when I first heard about coronavirus." People will talk about the silly things like the way Corona beer had to advertise that they had nothing to do with the virus. People will talk about the hard things like the way their lives were changed by lockdown orders and job losses. In the first weeks of the pandemic, millions of people filed for unemployment; the economy was savaged.

Schools were closed and graduations cancelled; parents became teachers, and teachers learned new ways to engage students online. People worried about the food supply and whether there was enough bandwidth for their online jobs. Health care workers and first responders will talk about the ways they waited helplessly for additional supplies of the kinds of things people had always taken for granted: hospital gowns and hand sanitizer, ventilators and hospital beds, the ability to touch their patients without fear of infection. Families will talk about the unspeakable sadness of being separated from their beloved who died alone. And liturgists and church leaders will talk about the ways that they worked to gather people in worship when people couldn't gather in public, and replaced the last rites for the dying with online communication.

The pandemic hit St. Gregory's slowly at first; we noticed subtle changes that quickly accelerated. On the first Sunday in March, only three children came to the service. On the second Sunday in March, we followed the bishop's pastoral direction that no one could drink from the shared chalice. On the third Sunday in March, we began our livestream of the liturgy. When I look back at the calendar of March, 2020, the beginning of the month looks like it always has: busy Sundays with two liturgies and classes for all ages, a memorial service in the afternoon, a choral concert. But the calendar goes still on March 15, every regular event marked "cancelled."

Our first livestream was held in the church building on March 15, 2020, forty-eight hours before the San Francisco health department ordered the city's lockdown, four days before the governor did the same for the whole state. I went to the church on the Friday before our livestream to set up the room for a different kind of worship. Facebook had been filled with colleagues and strangers sharing tips on how to create liturgy for a decentralized congregation. In the early days people asked all kinds of questions and posted all kinds of responses. "Is it okay for the priest to celebrate the eucharist, but not consume the bread and wine?" "What about consecrating bread and wine that people have at home?" "I've never done Morning Prayer, where does the sermon go?" I had questions too. "How the hell do we have a highly participatory liturgy when there's no one there to participate?"

St. Gregory's liturgy is built on a foundation that expects everyone present to share their experiences. People do this in all parts of the service. Before things changed in the pandemic, every Sunday had a consistent ordo. At the very beginning, our music director Sanford would say, "We're all the choir today, so sing boldly." We would invite children to come up and sprinkle incense on the hot coals of the brazier by the lectern. The choir would sit throughout the congregation, singing the hymns in four-part harmony, and we would invite everyone to sing whatever part fits their voice. After the sermon, people would stand and share their own stories. The intercessions were spoken spontaneously by members of the congregation as the Spirit and their desire called them forth. We would use ritual touch throughout the service, placing hands on shoulders for the two congregational dances we use and embracing each other in Christ's peace. People would linger over coffee hour and then take the liturgy with them, living it out for the week until they returned.

Trying to lean into these core values seemed impossible in the early days of the pandemic. It was easy enough to plan a liturgy where the presider would address the congregation, not necessarily expecting their response. This was the sort of liturgy that I had witnessed in many different places across the church, liturgy as a kind of one-way street that led to the dismissal. The presider drives the liturgy forward saying, "The Lord be with you," and the people predictably responding, "And also with you." That trope, both the text and the performance of the text, had become so engrained in Episcopalians that it was too often used to get people's attention in large gatherings: "The Lord be with you— And also with you—I just want to make a few announcements about where you can find the bathrooms." That performance raises the question of whether we believe in the evocative power of the ancient greeting to locate people's hearts in Christ's Spirit or if it's just good crowd control.

Language matters. The performance of the liturgy matters. Creating a Sunday morning, non-eucharistic liturgy was completely doable. Improvising the liturgy of Morning Prayer in a resonant way for the St. Gregory's community was something we'd done for decades. The script of the liturgy wasn't the problem when it came to streaming worship; the problem was the connection between worshippers that made the script come alive.

One of the ways that we nurture connection is with singing. Everything we sing is unaccompanied; hymns are sung in four-part harmony. When the presider chants the prayers, the congregation intones a note or chord. This intonation, called an *ison* in Eastern Christian worship, is a foundation to the presider's chant that actively gathers everyone in the prayer. The choir sits throughout the congregation to support the singing of the whole congregation; even those who are shy of singing can stay on pitch when a strong voice is near them. Because there is no accompaniment, the music director leads the singing using his face and body to urge people, setting tempo and pitch so that we can gather our voices in song. All of these practices are difficult, if not impossible, to do when we are not together in the same space for worship.

In the early days of the pandemic it felt like we were learning how to fly the airplane while we were still building it. I knew that I could build a script for streaming worship. I knew what the challenges were that we faced trying to interpret a highly participatory liturgy for the screen. As I scrolled through Facebook messages and various tweets from colleagues, I got a clearer sense of what a St. Gregory's streaming liturgy might look like. What I couldn't fully grasp was the technical challenge of moving my ideas out of my head and onto everyone's screens. Like many of my colleagues, I found the YouTube videos and web pages that offered tutorials on how to livestream worship. Since I am a digital immigrant and not a digital native, I had to watch videos multiple times and reread blog posts to understand both the concept of livestreaming and the technique. As the first Sunday of our livestreaming liturgy approached, I felt more and more dread. How could I master the technology?

My greatest failures in the liturgy result in my forgetting that I don't have to do everything on my own. Every Sunday, I encourage others to share leadership in worship; I truly believe that it is the best way to make church. But when I give in to dread, when my imagination is frozen by anxiety, I forget this. My best practices leave me. And although it is the truest thing about life in the Body of Christ, I don't quite believe that people will be able to help me. In my worst moments, I forget that people not only want to help me, they can do things better than I can.

Kyle Oliver has been an assisting priest at St. Gregory's since he and his wife Kristin Saylor moved to San Francisco in 2018. Along with the five other clergy who assist me in preaching and presiding at St. Gregory's, Kyle would lead the 8:30 service every few weeks. He was finishing his doctoral work, and Kristin was the director of formation at Grace Cathedral. I'm certain I had run into him at some large church gathering, but didn't really know that much about his work. Over the months, I gained a greater appreciation for his huge intellect, spiritual maturity, and unflappable ability to roll with whatever came. Unlike me, Kyle is a digital native. He also has experience in podcasting and live-streaming events.

The week before our livestream debut, feeling helpless, I emailed Kyle, "What do you think about coming over Sunday at 9:30 to help me with the 10:00 livestream? Completely up to you, no pressure." The fact that Kyle replied positively the next day was enough to ease me back from the edge of panic toward the center where Christ is all in all. Kyle's generous offering of his time and talents was a clear example of the liturgy as the people's work, a force that gathers us in one body.

The idea of liturgy being the work of the people comes from a particular interpretation of the Greek root of the word, *leitourgos*. In one interpretation, the stress is on *people* more than work; it carries a sense of people's right to have a part in the liturgy. We take this interpretation for granted. But the classic understanding of the word is more about *work* than people. In classical Greek *leitourgos* means one who discharges a public office at his own expense.[2] Say, for example, the bridge from downtown Athens to the suburbs is washed out in a storm. The *leitourgos* is the one who pays to repair the bridge so that everyone can get across town. For the *leitourgos*, it is the work that matters despite the cost; individual rights are forfeited for the sake of personal responsibility. In this understanding, the liturgy is what some of us do so that all of us can benefit; it is costly and is done for the common good.

When worship actively engages people in leadership for the common good, it is liturgy. When different individuals claim their authority and exercise it at their own cost, the liturgy shows the community something of the nature of Christ. The spirit of the liturgy is defined in the words of Paul's letter to the Philippians (2:5–7): "Let the same mind be in you that was in Christ Jesus,

---

2. James Strong, *Strong's Exhaustive Concordance of the Bible* (Peabody, MA: Hendrickson Publishers, 2007), 1644.

who, though he was in the form of God, did not regard equality
with God as something to be exploited, but emptied himself, taking the form of a slave, being born in human likeness." Sharing
both the authority and the cost of leadership recalls us to our corporate identity. When we practice liturgy as *leitourgos*, the common work of God's people is done by some of us for the sake of
the whole. This is the understanding of liturgy that serves a livestream worship service.

A group of six people gathered in St. Gregory's church building for our first livestream. Sanford sat by the Japanese temple bells that we ring to indicate silences after the readings and
sermon. Leesy, the church treasurer who regularly makes the
announcements, sat in a chair off camera. Brad had already been
assigned as a lay liturgical leader that day, so he and his husband
Brian joined us.

Kyle came before any of them. He walked into the church
still wearing his bike helmet, carrying what looked like a heavy
computer bag. "Where can I connect my laptop to an ethernet
port?" Although the church building is on our wireless network,
the upload would be much faster with a hardwired connection.

While he climbed up to the loft over the kitchen where the
base station was located, Sanford got his bells organized and Brad
rehearsed the long reading from John's gospel, "Jesus came to
a Samaritan city called Sychar. . . ." Leesy and I consulted on
the day's announcements: "I have to do the treasurer thing and
remind people to keep up with their pledge payments, but I'm
going to let people know they can postpone their payments if
they're out of work now." Kyle set up the laptop, turned on the
camera, and focused on me. I looked at myself on screen, among
my least favorite activities. I thought, "Why did I wear a brown
sweater? I look like a scary forest creature."

Kyle wore his wireless headphones and did a sound check. He
copied code from the Facebook Live feed to link the streaming
liturgy to our webpage. Every five minutes he'd shake his head,
"The link isn't working." I felt the familiar sense of panic over
things I can't control sneak up on me. Remarkably, I didn't step in

and try to fix something that was beyond my ken. We ran a test of the livestream; I improvised something to say to whomever was already watching, and I thought, "This is going to work, People are going to be able to connect in the liturgy."

The ten o'clock hour came. Sanford was going to begin the livestream chanting Psalm 95, which begins, "O come, let us sing to the Lord." He finished his improvised chant, and I stepped into frame and began the spoken part of the liturgy. The six of us sang, Brad read from John's gospel. I preached a sermon about loving our neighbors by staying physically apart from them. Leesy stepped up and made the day's announcements, and then we prayed. Throughout the livestream, people left comments in the chat line on Facebook Live, sharing a word after the reading and then intercessions in the silence of the prayers. "Living water." "Welling up." "For Donna who feels lonely." "For doctors and nurses in the pandemic." The end of the liturgy came, and I bid my people—scattered like grain upon the earth—Christ's peace. I didn't know what to do at the very end; I think I may have blown a kiss.

We were all silent for a moment, and then I took a deep breath, "We are going to make it. In fact, we're going to keep doing a livestream when this is all over." More than 400 people had stopped by our Facebook page during the livestream; we estimated more than 120 stayed for the whole liturgy. More than ninety comments were left in the chat line. It felt strange and relieving, and completely real. St. Gregory's Church had done what I didn't quite believe we could: we shared our distinct, highly participatory liturgy online.

It was clear that we were still in uncharted territory. The exhilaration of that first Sunday of streaming liturgy was dampened the next Sunday when Facebook Live crashed. Colleagues across the church shared the same experience; there just wasn't enough bandwidth to support all of the livestreaming liturgies being pushed out at 10:00 a.m. the next Sunday morning. But we managed to relocate everyone into a Zoom conference room, and the liturgy continued. Members of St. Gregory's stayed online after the liturgy to share their experiences in the pandemic. There were tears, and funny stories, and love shared freely from screen to screen.

But there was no bread and wine. One of the great griefs of the pandemic, one of the most consequential parts of physical distancing, was our inability to gather for the eucharist. In some congregations, videos of the mass were shared with people after the fact or livestreamed into their homes. And there were other innovations: I know more than one priest who gave communion to people who drove by in their cars. Bishops had to scramble and devise pastoral directions for a situation that none of us imagined: what happens to the liturgy when we cannot gather in the church building?

For our community, the answer was straightforward: we cannot have the eucharist if we cannot be together. Although some suggested consecrating the bread and wine at a distance, the words spoken in one place and the bread and wine in individual houses, it is not the consecratory prayer alone that makes the eucharist. The entire eucharistic liturgy—the gathering of the people, the proclamation of the gospel, bringing the needs of the world in prayer—all of these are where the presence of Christ is truly experienced. To consecrate the bread and wine of the eucharist apart from the people of God doesn't satisfy. It's the difference between watching Julia Child prepare a meal on TV and sitting down to dine with her.

The eucharist isn't magic. Christ doesn't slip into the bread and wine as a kind of sacred inoculation that changes the substance into his flesh and blood. Christ's Spirit is alive in us and throughout the universe. It is in the act of remembering him, and faithfully claiming his Spirit is in our spirits that the bread and wine are his Body and Blood, transforming us to become as he is. We are transformed by his Spirit even if physical distancing protocols separate us from the bread and wine. The Spirit of Christ filling all things leads us into future hope, whether we have the bread and wine with us or not. Our whole lives—past, present, and yet to come—are the places where we participate in the mystery of Christ's body and blood. And when the bread and wine are far from us, the living Spirit of Christ remains with us.

The eucharist gives us the energy to live as Christ's Body in the world. When we are apart from the bread and wine—and each other—we continue to live eucharistically. Every time we do the works of Christ in the world, we make eucharist. The ultimate gift of Jesus, the gift that he brings to us from the cross, is to make us his eucharistic body. It is as this living body that we find our way into the world, serving those who need us the most: the lonely, sick, frightened, weak, and desperate. This is what we can do when we cannot gather at Christ's altar and receive the bread and the wine. And it is all we have to do to find the grace we usually receive in the eucharist.

Everything about the church has been changed by the COVID-19 pandemic; we can never return to the way things were before. People we love have died. Churches that were struggling before the pandemic have closed. Clergy have taken early retirement. But people continue to connect. We are finding new ways to engage each other in prayer and spiritual practice. St. Gregory's online Morning Prayer service continues to meet Monday–Friday. I stay in closer touch with my parishioners who still can't manage to leave their homes even though the lockdown has been lifted. We long to return to the table and receive there the bread and wine that are Christ's Body and Blood. And I remember the prayer that my friend Mark Childers shared at the end of another in a long series of Zoom meetings, taken from the Armed Forces prayer book, a prayer for those who cannot draw near to Christ's table:

> In union, O Lord, with your faithful people at every altar of your Church, where the Holy Eucharist is now being celebrated. I desire to offer you praise and thanksgiving. I remember your death, Lord Christ; I proclaim your resurrection; I await your coming in glory. And since I cannot receive you today in the physical presence of my community, I beseech you

to come spiritually into my heart. Cleanse and strengthen me with your grace, Lord Jesus, and let me never be separated from you. May I live in you, and you in me, in this life and the life to come. Amen.

This is what I'm learning about the connection between life and liturgy . . .

God wants to be known in our lives, which makes our lives precious.

The most shadowed times of our lives may be the birthplace of hope.

My liturgical leadership is only as powerful as my willingness to be vulnerable.

Forgiveness comes alive in the liturgy when it is shared between all people.

Everything we have ever known about church is changing.

Where in your life does the liturgy ground you and connect you to other people?

CHAPTER 2

Improvisation, Disruption, and Liturgy

The Gospel Plow

In the summer of 2019, I learned about improvisation in a surprising place: the Cathedral Church of Christ in Liverpool. It was a transformative experience and gave me new ways to consider how to hack the prayer book.

David and Debra had agreed to pick me up from the train station in Liverpool and drop me off at the cathedral. I'd already heard about the grandeur of the building when I was on retreat at the Community of the Resurrection in Mirfield, West Yorkshire. It seemed like everyone who heard I was invited by Paul Bayes, the bishop of Liverpool, to participate in the ordination service at the cathedral said the same thing, "You know, it's the largest enclosed space in Europe." I've had some experience of cathedrals in my life. I began professional ministry at Christ Church Cathedral in Houston, Texas. Twelve years there, doing every job from youth minister to head of staff, had brought me close to all the predictable aspects of large-scale liturgy. I had been in charge of liturgies at Grace Cathedral in San Francisco, and years before had carried a processional umbrella up and down the aisles of the Cathedral of St. Peter and St. Paul in Washington, D.C. I thought I knew everything there was to know about large-scale liturgy in cathedral churches. I assumed that the largest enclosed space in Europe would host a larger-than-life liturgy—just more loud organ and long silent walks from choir stall to pulpit and back again.

I'd come to England as a part of my sabbatical in 2019. After spending a few days in Oxford visiting friends and walking in the storybook beauty of the university, I went for three weeks of peace and icon painting in a monastery. The stop in Liverpool was an afterthought. Bishop Paul had visited my church in San Francisco eighteen months before. After all of my plans were made, I thought to email and see if there was any time that I might come and see him in his diocese. Paul Bayes is a remarkable man, one of those Evangelical Anglicans who have come to embrace the reign of God's justice that includes full inclusion for LGBTQ+ folks. When he was in San Francisco, I felt an immediate bond with him. His invitation to come and vest, process in, and join in laying hands with the other presbyters from the Liverpool Diocese was an honor.

David and Debra drove up to the front of the cathedral. The building was vast, all rosy-brown stone and twentieth-century gothic architecture—a building on an imperial scale. It was designed by the architect Giles Gilbert Scott, who also designed Britain's iconic red phone box. The cathedral was built for a different era of the church, an era where everyone was assumed to be both Christian and faithful in attending the liturgy. It had taken seventy-four years to complete, and by the time it was finished the church in Britain had become something very different— and so had Liverpool. When the plans for the gigantic cathedral had been drawn up, Liverpool was a vital business and shipping center, the second city of England. By the time the building was completed, it was depopulated and struggling for its identity. Still, Liverpool Cathedral kept rising higher and higher over the city, a testament to an idea of church that had simply disappeared.

As I approached the front doors, I thought I knew what it would be like. I knew cathedrals; I expected that the liturgy would be a mix of spectacle and mistakes. I thought I knew what would happen. And as soon as I walked in the doors, I began to see that I was mistaken. It was a day that I learned about improvisation and liturgy.

Just inside the cathedral hung a globe of the earth, twenty-three feet in diameter, illuminated from within, spinning slowly about twenty feet above my head. Entitled *Gaia*, it is a work by

Luke Jerram, installed as a part of Liverpool's River Festival in early spring of 2019. I wasn't surprised to find art in a cathedral; that is one of the functions of these mega-churches. But the scale of the piece, the intensity of the encounter with it just as I entered the building, surprised and delighted me. I learned later that more than 200,000 people had come to see it, to stand beneath the earth in joy and delight. Beyond *Gaia*, the rest of the building stretched on and on toward the altar. Behind it, further east and more remote, were the choir and high altar. There was more than enough space for the fourteen ordinands, their families, mentors, supervisors, and friends—as well as the seventy-five or so diocesan clergy who attended. And there was me.

The bishop's assistant found me and handed me a dark briefcase, "Your vestments are inside. It's red stoles." She walked quickly away, a thousand details to attend to. I went downstairs and found the dressing room where I joined the other clergy, opened the briefcase, took out the white alb and red stole, and got dressed. I knew no one. An older priest, retired but still active in justice work, was my handler. "Just follow me, and everything will be fine." I followed him out of the basement, up the stairs, to the back and lined up, two by two like we were going into Noah's ark. And then, there was Bishop Paul. "I'm so glad you could be here," he said as we embraced me. "Just follow this guy, and everything will be fine."

I'm used to following instructions when it comes to the liturgy. That is the way priests are trained to preside in liturgy: just follow the rubrics, say the words, and everything will be fine. But it isn't fine, not always. There are times when priests feel like we are battered between a kind of mindless repetition of words we can't quite grasp and occasionally being so caught up in the words we can barely see them for the tears in our eyes. The vocation to lead people in prayer is exhilarating and confusing. Leading God's people in worship is the greatest privilege I can imagine and yet sometimes feels like playing make-believe. I remember times where I have spoken the solemn words of the eucharistic prayer at a cathedral altar while thinking about what I would have for lunch that afternoon. I remember putting on my resting priest face during weddings where I couldn't stand the thought of so much money being spent on flowers and clothes that nobody really wanted to wear. Following instructions sometimes seems as good as it gets.

That's the problem with thoughtlessly following instructions: it renders the liturgy as just "as good as it gets." Simply following instructions safely sets the one who leads the prayers apart from the power of the prayers; it makes us into little more than mouth-pieces and meat puppets of sacred texts. Still, I believe that the structure of prayer matters. The structure matters because some-times I need it to carry me through seasons of dryness and doubt. The rubrics matter because they give God's people some common place within which to make our common prayer. The words of the prayer book mean that I do not have to carry God's people through their prayers based on my personality and my gifts; I can trust in the generations who have come before me, who have said these same prayers, to stand with me when I don't really believe what I'm saying. We need all of the stuff that gives us structure, but structure is not enough; following instructions is not enough; it is not as good as it gets. If those who lead the liturgy are going to continue to grow, if our spirits are going to soar in the liturgy, we have to turn from structure to improvisation.

The ordination service continued. From the side where I sat with the other clergy, I could see most of the liturgical action. There was also a video monitor, where I could watch more closely the details of the liturgy. When priests are ordained, the custom is for all of the priests in attendance to come forward and join the bishop in laying hands on the ordinands. I took my place in the back of the crowd of priests, stretching out my hand and placing it on the shoulder of the women in front of me each time Bishop Paul said the prayer and placed his hands on another ordinand's head. As the candidates traded places before the bishop, there would be a minor rearrangement of people; the supervisors of the ordinands would squeeze to the front. There were smiles and small, awkward bits of conversation as we moved about. This was a kind of improvisation: making space for the human contact that matters in the midst of larger-than-life ritual.

Toward the end of the service, after the ordinations, the eucharistic prayer, the communion of the people—just before the post-communion prayer—there was a moment of silence. Bishop Paul stood at the center holding the vast liturgical space. I looked down at my printed order of service to find the words of the prayer we would all join, but the silence continued a beat or two longer than I expected. I looked up and saw the bishop was in prayer, his eyes closed and his hands resting on the altar. Then it happened: a moment of liturgical improvisation that took my breath away. In the midst of the congregation, in the center of the gigantic cathedral, Bishop Paul began to sing:

> Well, I got my hands on the Gospel plow
> And I wouldn't take nothin' for my journey now
> Keep your hand on the plow of God
> Hold on, hold on.

His voice was strong, but not overly loud. He continued to hold the space as he continued to sing, and it occurred to me what he was doing: this was his pastoral charge to the newly ordained. It was also his prophetic word to the whole people. It could have been a moment of high kitsch: an English bishop in a state-sponsored cathedral singing a song from the African American spiritual tradition. It was a moment of improvisation that could have gone so wrong, but it didn't. The act of improvisation fit the moment, and the individual, and the context perfectly.

As it relates to the liturgy, improvisation is about adding to what is known in the moment of "performing" the liturgy while attending to the essential meaning of the prayers. Improvisation is not just doing what you want to do; it is not about novelty for the sake of novelty. Far from obscuring the core meaning of the liturgy, the best improvisation seems to fit in the flow of what has come before it. At its best, liturgical improvisation may not even be noticed as such by the assembly. Commenting on musical improvisation, Lee B. Brown writes:

> . . . some improvisations may seem predictable just because
> they unfold with such striking musical "rightness." That they
> do so may seem uncanny, indeed surprising—surprising for
> an improvisation, that is. By contrast, it would be strange to
> describe a piece of music as sounding surprisingly "right" for a
> piece of composed music.[1]

In contrast, novelty in the liturgy is most notable for being
noticed; it's like a speed bump on the roadway of prayer that stops
the energy and flow of the liturgy.

Improvisation is always a surprise; the surprise of an improviser's rightness is no less surprising to the improvisers themselves.
The rightness of improvisation is realized in the moment of the
action itself, not just in comparison to what has come before.
Improvisers are primarily interested in making something new
out of what has been done and said before. When problems arise
in the liturgy, liturgical improvisers work to close the gap between
what has been known previously and what has yet to be revealed.
Improvisation includes facing the problems inherent in the creative act, not ignoring them. Improvisation accepts the world that
is with all of its surprises, limitations, and promises. Improvisation recognizes that what wants to be communicated is not bound
to what has come before, but attends to what the example of the
past has to say to the current moment of experience.

Keith Sawyer is the Morgan Distinguished Professor in Edu-
cation Innovation at the University of North Carolina at Chapel
Hill. His field covers creativity, innovation, and learning; he also
writes about improvisation. Sawyer identifies five characteristics
of improvisation: process over product, problem-finding instead
of problem-solving, similarity to everyday language use, collaboration as central, and using the ready-made.[2]

1. Lee B. Brown, "Musical Works, Improvisation, and the Principle of Continuity," *The Journal of Aesthetics and Art Criticism* 54, no. 4 (Autumn 1996): 364.

2. R. Keith Sawyer, "Improvisation and the Creative Process: Dewey, Collingwood, and the Aesthetics of Spontaneity," *The Journal of Aesthetics and Art Criticism* 58, no. 2 (Spring 2000): 152.

Improvisation emphasizes creative process rather than an end goal or product. When it comes to improvisation, what matters is what happens in the present moment, not what we will have as a final outcome. People who improvise don't think about whether or not they are doing things the "right way" if that means knowing how everything will end up well. Instead, improvisers are keenly attuned to the moment in which they are active. Improvisers pay attention to what is happening around them: what they are experiencing in the task at hand and how that experience is being influenced by the other people in the room with them. Improvisers recognize that what is going on in any given moment is exactly what needs to be happening to energetically move the action forward—even if it isn't clear what the next action might be.

Each moment of the liturgy is a moment in which improvisation might be welcomed. This is because there is always a subtext to the liturgy. The words and actions in any given moment are dominant, but they are not the only variables at play. Other variables include the presider's own energy and the energy of the congregation, the physical space within which the ritual action is contained, the larger issues of society that surround the liturgy, and the not infrequent mistakes and moments of happenstance that occur in social gatherings. If we don't attend to these variables, the subtexts of the gathering, then the liturgy can be diminished or distorted. When the leader is attuned to these variables, then openings to improvisation become clearer.

Bishop Paul's improvisation at the end of the ordination was possible because he was attuned to the moment. Instead of moving thoughtlessly from one ritual event to the next, he knew the context and the community in which he was presiding. He was able to improvise, because he was deeply rooted in the energy of the community and the significance of the moment. He was also aware of his creative agency and the authority that is always shared by the congregation with the presider of the liturgy. Although he'd been thinking of the song before he sang it, he was as surprised as the congregation was by what happened. There was something in that moment that simply called the words of the song from the background to the foreground of the moment. The word that was planted in his imagination was creatively unleashed without knowing what would happen next. Notice these kinds of openings for improvisation in liturgy; sometimes they are taken up and sometimes they are ignored.

Problem Finding vs. Problem Solving

I was visiting a local parish one Sunday morning. The congregation of forty-five people included a family with three young daughters. They came into the service after the opening acclamation—something that isn't at all unusual for a young family. They took their seats two pews ahead of me. Throughout the liturgy the two older girls would read or draw, and occasionally would ask one of their parents a question. I'm used to children in worship, so the sound of their young voices was not at all intrusive; I was glad that a family with young children managed to make it to the service.

The liturgy continued, and I continued to observe what was happening. A part of the liturgical subtext was clear to me: silence was privileged over interruption—an orderly service was expected by the people in charge of the liturgy. I noticed that the parents kept trying to quiet their daughters, and the children kept trying to find a place of engagement in the adult-centered liturgy. When the priest went to the altar and began to say the eucharistic prayer, one of the girls quickly stepped into the center aisle, standing and facing the altar. Again, the subtext was clear to me: the child couldn't see what was happening over the back of the adult-sized pew in front of her, and she imagined a solution to what was blocking her. I looked at the parents. They seemed a little panicked that their daughter had crossed the boundary from pew to aisle, breaking an unspoken norm of liturgical behavior. I thought, "This is the moment that matters. This is the moment when they decide to let the girl access the liturgy on her own terms, or they decide to conform her to the adult world of staying in place." It was a moment ripe for improvisation.

Unfortunately, from my perspective, one of the parents reached out and grabbed the girl's arm and brought her back into the pew. What might have happened? The presider might have noticed the girl standing in the aisle, paused the prayer, and invited her to come and stand with him at the altar. One of the parents might have joined the girl in the center aisle, maybe kneeling down to share in the prayer at the child's eye level. Or, maybe an elder member of the congregation might have noticed the girl, taken her by the hand, and led her to the open space in front of the church, close enough to see what was happening. If the process of the liturgy had been privileged over the product of it, any of these options might have been pursued. Instead, the most important thing seemed to be doing the liturgy the "right way." If the energy is only directed to the end goal, we miss many invitations to grace and improvisation.

Improvisation puts an emphasis on creative processes that are problem-finding rather than problem-solving.[3] These two phenomena are distinguished by where our attention is placed. Problem-solving processes have a clear idea in mind. In the liturgy, a problem-solving orientation is getting from the opening hymn to the final dismissal without too many hiccups. In my experience, this typifies most liturgy and liturgical instruction. I once participated in a cathedral procession that was deemed a triumph because the last member of the line arrived in place just as the last note of the organ sounded. I saw the woman in charge of the acolytes actually clapping her hands in glee because there was a successful ending to a complicated ritual action—all of which is fine, but leaves little opportunity for improvisation.

A problem-finding approach to the liturgy is one that is aware of what is happening in every moment as the liturgy progresses, and sees each moment as a chance for something beautiful to be realized by the congregation. For those who improvise, what matters is paying attention to what is going on in the liturgy, looking for the openings in the liturgy that will let in more

---

3. Ibid.

light. The liturgical leader who chooses to improvise must remain aware of what is actually happening in the room, not just what she or he imagines should be happening to achieve a predetermined ending. Sometimes it is the liturgical mistake that invites a new expression of grace. A cardinal rule of improvisation is that you have to work with what you have, which requires remaining aware in the course of the liturgy.

Bishop Paul's improvisation was an example of problem-finding in the liturgy. As is sometimes the case, the preacher at the ordination was not the bishop. Although the ordination sermon was fine and it reflected well on the occasion in which we'd gathered, it was not the bishop's proclamation to the ordinands. He found the problem: his word needing to be spoken in the midst of the assembly. It wasn't a problem-solving liturgical action: he went off script, it wasn't clear how much of the song would be sung, and there was a risk that his singing might go badly. But he took the risk, and the moment revealed something new in the midst of the liturgical action. In my experience, there are always such moments in the liturgy, finding problems that present opportunities for improvisation. The COVID-19 pandemic provided us with other opportunities for problem-finding improvisation.

Saint Gregory's had been gathering for worship online since the third Sunday in Lent; we had managed to find a rhythm of worship that worked. "That felt like us," a member posted on our Facebook sharing page. Many of my colleagues either recorded or livestreamed their services from church buildings, a few vested leaders standing six feet apart from each other in otherwise empty buildings. I made the decision that during the lockdown our liturgies would be livestreamed from participants' homes. I believed that staying out of the church building communicated to people the seriousness of our situation. It also presented us with creative challenges, something that St. Gregory's people are not unfamiliar with.

Good Friday in 2020 took place on the twenty-fourth day of the COVID-19–inspired shutdown of San Francisco. Like all of our liturgies, the Good Friday service is highly participatory and relies on a great deal of physical touch. It ends, as I shared in chapter 1, as we walk from one end of the building to the other, chanting Psalm 22 and laying flowers at the burial icon of Christ. The problems presented by a shelter-in-place order were massive; the list of things we could not do far exceeded those that we could. I talked to members of the parish, as well as to colleagues in the diocese, about how we might improvise the Good Friday liturgy so that it would "feel like us." A member of my clergy colleague group, Phil Brochard, shared that his parish, All Souls in Berkeley, planned on asking people at home to strip bare the places from where they were watching the liturgy. It was just the kind of embodied liturgical practice that I thought would work for us.

I had asked people to prepare a place in their home where they could log in to our Holy Week liturgies—a holy corner that everyone watching the live feed could see and enjoy. Beginning on Palm Sunday, people sat with green branches and pieces of red fabric. For the Maundy Thursday liturgy, I encouraged people to gather at tables set with their favorite dishes. In daily emails that I sent during Holy Week, I asked them to prepare their homes. On Friday I wrote,

> Remember to prepare for Good Friday by making sure your holy corner is adorned with whatever signs of beauty you have: icons, branches, flowers, and somber fabrics. And please remember to have a candle with you. At the opening of the service, we will light the candle as a sign of Christ's presence with us even in the most shadowed times of our lives. At the end of the liturgy we will strip away the signs of beauty in remembrance of Jesus's death on the cross. But we will keep our candles burning: the light never leaves us.

All told, there were twenty people leading the service in places from Pacifica, California to Hutchinson, Minnesota. Two choir members in one household sang the hymns, and five people in four locations sang the Passion. The liturgy began as it does every year: singing out our love to Jesus. As the lead voice changed, that person's image would take center screen. We listened to the scriptures' promise of God's mercy in the midst of the worst thing the human imagination can devise. We offered prayers for one another and the world, five different priests singing the solemn collects in five different places. Then we came to the moment of the biggest problem-solving improvisation. I said,

> Normally, this would be the time that we all go to the altar and leave our flowers for Christ's burial. Tonight, we are apart from each other looking forward to the time when we can gather together face to face. Instead of leaving flowers, I ask you to clear the holy corner in your home where you have gathered to join us online. Take away the flowers and fabrics, the branches and other things that you have had in place. But don't blow out your candle; the light shines in the darkness, and the light never leaves us.

Four separate voices chanted the verses of Psalm 22 and we each, in our separate places, began to strip bare the places where we sat. I removed the three icons behind me, took down the brown and gold cloths, and took my place in front of a bare wall for the conclusion of the service. It was not the same as our usual devotions on Good Friday but it was real, beautiful, and felt completely like us. It was a moment in which everyone had to improvise, finding the problem that they could address in ways that were woven into the liturgy. I never had a class in seminary on "What to do when a pandemic makes you livestream Good Friday," but it wasn't necessary: what we needed in the moment was already with us.

Everything Is a Gift

Human beings are always improvising when it comes to conversation. We step into conversations not knowing what has already been said and find a way to join in. Or we meet an old friend for coffee and simply talk about the events of the day, or week, or year, seldom sharing our narratives from a prepared script. One person says something, which reminds us of something in our experience that we share, then the other person shares an experience, and so on. Conversation is enjoyable precisely because we do not know where it is going; sometimes a conversation becomes particularly memorable because it goes in a direction we never imagined. The same energy that permeates our everyday conversations enters into the creation of liturgy. What matters in the liturgy is recognizing that the leader and the congregation are always in dialogue, always attending to what the other person says and does. The opposite is like the old joke about the bishop who goes up to preach and, looking at her watch, notices that it has stopped working. She says, "There's something wrong with this thing," to which the people reply, "and also with you."

Bishop Paul's improvisation relied on the responsiveness of the congregation, even though the assembly didn't join in singing. Perhaps because his singing was a solo, the bishop took another step into improvisation. After he had sung, he paused a moment and without introduction led the people in singing something familiar:

> Praise God from whom all blessings flow;
> Praise him all creatures here below;
> Praise him above ye heavenly hosts;
> Praise Father, Son, and Holy Ghost.

As he began to sing, more and more voices joined him; harmony was added, and the sound of voices increased. There was a need for a corporate act at this moment of the liturgy, and the bishop took another improvisational risk, trusting that the conversational ability of the congregation would meet his call. Another cleric told me more about the intersection of everyday conversation and improvisation.

Les Carpenter is an Episcopal priest who has practiced improv performance for more than ten years. He started doing improv as a part of his self-care when he was ordained; very early in his ministry, he found it to be an antidote to all the problems that come along in working for the church. Eventually, Les started an improv theater group at his church. Every week between four and twenty people would show up. Each week, he would direct or participate in the improvised scenes. All ages would participate. I asked Les what the effect of improv had on his congregation. He said, "I know that one of the kids is probably going to become a priest as a result."

Les describes the pleasure that he found in improv by saying, "In improv, everything is a gift." You show up with yourself and nothing else but the presumption that the world in which we live is one shot through with grace. As in improv, so in liturgy: everything is a gift. Thus, the conversational quality of improvisation in the liturgy assumes that each one present is there for the sake of the larger conversation in which the whole community is participating. Each member of the assembly is present as a participant in God's grace and as an avenue for encountering God's grace anew. Each person gives of the grace that God pours out on all creation. Likewise, in improv performance, you give and you receive and everyone gets to participate in this dynamic; this is the genius of improv, and it is also the genius of everyday conversation.

When we engage in conversation we don't use a script to guide us: we just start talking, welcoming our conversation partners to change the course of the conversation as they see fit. Conversation is continually being negotiated among the conversation partners, so we rarely worry where the conversation will lead us. In everyday conversation, we seldom try to stop the conversation dead in its tracks by offering random non sequiturs. And if something sounds peculiar in daily conversation, we have the opportunity to seek clarification from our conversation partner. It is the same in improvisation. "Everything is a gift," Les repeats, "the gift of improv is *yes—and*." The "yes-and" means that the performers work to keep moving forward in the scene. This calls each performer to attend to the action that is taking place in the moment, as well as the standard conventions of human interaction. I asked Les what kills improv: "Denial. If one person doesn't respond to the other person—if they reject the imagined reality that they've been given in the scene. Then the scene is over." Les describes improv and liturgy as "play." Each phenomenon is about the delight that the community takes in the yes-and of the moment. Both improv performance and the church's liturgy work with what is available to create a transformative moment where grace can be recognized anew.

Les shared a story about a liturgy in which he participated years before his ordination, a story that describes the yes-and. It was a gathering of teens who had been tasked with planning and leading the eucharistic liturgy. The group worked together to write the intercessions and eucharistic prayer, they imagined new ways of responding to the Word of scripture, and they took charge of the ordained and their roles in the service. They did not attend as closely to the rubrics of the liturgy as more seasoned ordained leaders might have. At the moment for the reading of the gospel, an event that prayer book rubrics designate for an ordained person, a young man carried the gospel book into the midst of the assembly for the reading, followed by a vested deacon. The deacon assumed that she would be reading the gospel, until the young man announced, "The Holy Gospel of our Lord Jesus Christ according to John." At that point this deacon made the improvisational choice of yes-and; she removed her stole and put it over the teen reader's shoulder, wrapping it around him in the manner of a deacon.

This ordained woman recognized that the liturgy was like a conversation: she expected it to go one way—the yes—and it went another—the and. Instead of being hemmed in by the rubrics, she took the chance of engaging play and improvisation in the liturgy. Her ability to say yes-and allowed the liturgy to evolve and move forward in a way that was just and full of beauty. As two people in an everyday conversation might, she did not deny the action, but made something new so that the conversation might move forward. Some might describe this moment as a liturgical failure. But as Les says, "Failure is what makes it interesting."

All of this leads to the next characteristic to consider in liturgical improvisation: the importance of collaboration. Within the liturgy there are many people with whom the presider may collaborate: fellow ministers vested for leadership, members of the congregation who are familiar with the regular rhythm of the service, those among the assembly who have specific roles like

ushering. There are also collaborators who are less obvious in liturgy: pre-verbal children, first-time visitors without experience of
ritual-heavy liturgy, unhoused people who may experience emotional distress, and a thousand others who come and enrich the
ritual life of the church. Each of these may be the mediator of
God's grace in the action of the liturgy. Collaboration is a significant quality of improvisation because the liturgy is always a public
event: whomever shows up for the service is a part of making the
service. Even if it is just responding "and also with you," the liturgy is necessarily a collaboration among participants.

I suspect that for many ordained people, collaboration is challenging because it requires vulnerability. I'm a fan of vulnerability
in the same way that I'm a fan of flu shots: it's necessary to operate in the very public work of liturgical leadership. Sometimes
vulnerability hurts, and it means that we really do need each other
in order to improvise. I asked Les about his experience of denial
in improv performance. When everyone is gathered to do improv,
why in the world would someone seek to undermine the performance? Les replied, "It's all about protective behavior; trying
to protect yourself from vulnerability and looking bad. You lose
your courage and you go to denial, and then the game is over." He
paused, and then added, "And everyone does it."

We all lose our courage from time to time, and sometimes
when we lose courage we turn away from collaboration and go
to control. Seeking to control oneself—and the assembly—in the
liturgy is seldom a good idea, but it does offer the superficial hope
of safety. Yet seeking to exercise control in the liturgy flies in the
face of the community's need to be made real by the liturgy. Collaboration in the liturgy gives us the opportunity to practice the
values of heaven in the midst of the messiness of human social
gatherings. We need collaboration in the liturgy to be the church,
especially when it is uncomfortable.

Bishop Paul's improvisation—singing a spiritual in the midst
of a perfectly respectable liturgy—made him extremely vulnerable.
His voice is not professionally trained; it wasn't bad, but it wasn't
a professional performance. When he began to sing I had no idea

what might happen next; I didn't know if I was supposed to join in singing, or just listen, or do something else. In large part, it was his vulnerability that invited newness in the moment. It was not necessary for the action of the liturgy to move forward, and nobody would have missed the bishop's improvisation if he had decided against it. But the trust that he held in the community to meet his vulnerability with love allowed him to collaborate in the creation of the liturgy with the community. The congregation's singing in the second half of his improvisation demonstrated that we were willing to meet Bishop Paul in the midst of his vulnerability: we were all collaborating in a liturgical improvisation.

My experience tells me that collaboration is essential in liturgy. Even when the presider is just trying to get from the opening hymn to the final dismissal, liturgy is always relational: not knowing what might happen requires attention to the real, lived experience of the liturgy. I learned about this kind of attention a few years ago when I was teaching liturgics in the Diocese of Minnesota. Since 2015, I have taught low-residency students preparing for ordination either in December or January. It's really cold in Minnesota in December and January. I woke up one Sunday morning, and it was -14 degrees. With the wind chill, it was -30 degrees. The cold was like a monster that surrounded me and then got inside of me. A few seconds in that cold and I could feel the hairs in my nose freeze. Bundled up as I was, it hurt to be in that freezing air.

I talked to my friend Devon about what people do when it gets this cold. She told me that people buddy-up when it's freezing. When it gets that cold, you aren't supposed to go outside alone. If the door locks behind you, or if you can't find your car keys and you're alone, you will die. You have to have someone who can be there for you. And although I was never in any real danger of freezing to death, I did have to stand in the cold while my friend backed her car away from a snow bank so I could get in. Although it was no more than thirty seconds, I had that feeling of hopeless cold permeating my body. I thought, "If she drives off and leaves me here alone, I will die." In weather that cold, people have a unique grasp of what it means to deeply need one another. Deep cold is an optic through which to look at collaboration and improvisation in the liturgy.

Les calls improvisation "Collaborative Discovery." Our need for another person, any person, is at the heart of improvisation. I think it's a mistake to imagine that this need has to be grounded in our commonality, or similar interests, or shared cultural habits. Instead, it is precisely our differences that make liturgical improvisation so vital and so transformative. If the liturgy means nothing else, it means that despite the differences between us, we desperately need one another. What enlivens the liturgy is the recognition that we are connected to each other not by our own preferences but by the desire of God. So improvisation in the liturgy involves two phenomena that make us vulnerable: desire and need. This is costly. It means that my individual needs and abilities are always relative to yours. Collaboration urges me to live with the other and love the other, because the other person reveals something of God in the liturgy.

Collaboration in the liturgy means that everything matters: your body and my body, your ability and mine, your vision and hope and longing, as well as my own. It is our mutual connection as this great, mystical body engaged in the praise of God that matters. It is our connection that matters, not whether or not we are the same or whether or not we have the same liturgical taste. It isn't that one of us is right and one of us is wrong. The only thing that matters is the power that continues to draw us together into one body, which is always the Holy Spirit of God. When it comes to collaboration, what ultimately matters is our need.

What We Need We Have

A few years ago, I was passing out the bread during communion at the Easter Vigil at St. Gregory's. We always have a lot of visitors at the Vigil. I came to a man I knew who had brought a couple of friends to the liturgy. I gave him the bread saying, "the Body of Christ." Then I went to his first guest and did the same thing. Then I came to his second guest with the bread saying, "the Body of Christ." He put his hands up in a gesture of STOP and said, "I don't do carbs," which completely threw me. The opportunity for collaboration just melted away from me, and I couldn't figure out a meaningful way of improvising in the moment. So, I just said "amen" and moved to the next person.

That's a funny story of encountering strange bread in community, of being invited into improvisation, and feeling that the invitation to collaboration was inaccessible. But it's also a story about one of the things that closes down collaboration: denial based on consumer choice. Wanting something else when everyone is getting bread and wine is a kind of improvisational denial. Wanting things to go my way irrespective of the others in the liturgy blocks collaboration and stops the energy of the service. It is not the case that the other person's wanting something else is a bad thing; it's just that when we're at play in the liturgy, we are each dependent on the other as creative agents. So, denial based in consumer choice takes the sign of God's power to knock down the barriers that divide us and turns it into a joke. Each one of us is going to be tempted by some form of denial—that belief that what I want is more important than what the whole assembly needs to create the liturgy, which tells me that the liturgy cannot be created without continually attending to our need for collaboration.

The experience of God's wisdom makes us crave more of it. The liberation that God longs to give us, the generosity of God that is eternally being renewed in God's love, is present in every moment of the liturgy. Which is why the liturgy matters: we meet each other on a level field, and all we have to do is show up. Unless you don't do carbs. Or if you don't like people who have different opinions than yours. Or if you have a habit of "otherizing" folks of different races or nationalities or genders. Or if you already have it all figured out and just need to have your current beliefs confirmed. Or if you don't have time for the mess of other human beings. Collaboration in the liturgy matters because it puts us into relationship with people on the basis of God's wisdom and not our own choices.

Improvisation does not mean that anything goes; there has to be an original source that is a container for the lively work we do as liturgical improvisers. The improvisation that we seek in liturgy is only as good as our understanding of the tradition in which the liturgy was formed. As I tell my students, "Before you break the rules, you have to know the rules." The traditional material that provides the structure in which we do improvisation is called the "ready-made." The ready-made could be familiar tropes or well-loved traditions. For example, singing "Silent Night" on Christmas Eve while kneeling is a ready-made for Episcopalians. This ready-made is trying to increase a sense of reverence and beauty in the encounter with Christ's Incarnation. A liturgist might improvise around the ready-made by replacing the organ accompaniment with the original performance version. In the original, the priest and hymn writer Joseph Mohr played the guitar and sang the hymn with Franz Xaver Gruber, the choir master who wrote the melody. A gentler accompaniment would change the sense of reverence and beauty that people love in this liturgical ready-made.

The ready-made also includes actions that are discovered in the course of improvisation and are then applied in new ways in the liturgy. Paul of Tarsus gives us a good example of this in his pastoral instruction to the church in Corinth. The specific pastoral crisis that he addresses concerns the sharing of food at the ritual meal; rich people are coming early and eating everything, leaving the poor with nothing. He encourages the Corinthians to look beyond their personal needs and to remember the needs of the weaker members of the group. He conflates this memory of the poor with the memory of Jesus's own gift of life and freedom, given to them in his passion, death, and resurrection. Paul uses the ready-made to create a new liturgical norm. In remembering the poor and Jesus's actions for their sake, Paul says that in the liturgy the group's self-understanding is transformed; they are no longer seeking their own good, but have become a single body. It is as a body that the group is properly related in the liturgy and performing their identity as followers of Christ.

Improvising on a liturgical ready-made relies on the community's shared memory in order for it to be effective. This shared memory is one of the factors that holds the community of the church together. The shared memory, what Paul of Tarsus calls *anamnesis*, is always an active remembering. It is much more than a cognitive exercise of pulling together facts about a past event. Anamnesis is an embodied experience that brings the thing being remembered into the present. Anamnesis is a Greek term used in the Septuagint, the Greek translation of the Hebrew scriptures, to translate the Hebrew *zikkaron*, which means "memorial" or "remembrance." *Zikkaron* is the word used to define the Day of Passover for the Hebrew people: "This day shall be a day of remembrance for you. You shall celebrate it as a festival to the Lord; throughout your generations you shall observe it as a perpetual ordinance" (Exodus 12:14). In the annual celebration of the Passover, the people are instructed to claim, through remembrance, the actions of their ancestors and of God in delivering them from slavery into freedom. Again, this is not simply a cognitive exercise; it is standing with the ancestors in their deliverance from slavery into freedom.

Anamnesis is not only about memories past; it projects the community into the future with a sense of hope and trust. The future into which anamnesis remembers is the life of God. Because God's promise of freedom is given to all, even those not yet born may hope to be delivered from slavery and inherit the freedom that God desires for all beings. If a goal of the liturgy is to engage anamnesis, then improvisation is imperative. Even if using precisely the same words and material items in precisely the same way as previous generations, a contemporary liturgy will differ from the original iteration. This is because anamnesis is not just about information transmission; it is about the conscious appropriation of the assembly of God's people as the Body of Christ willingly participating in the liturgy.

Bishop Paul's improvisation clearly relied on the ready-made. He sang a piece of music that was not only well known to him, but also reflected the larger life of his diocese and its commitment to justice. Liverpool has been in a partnership with the Diocese of Virginia in the United States and the Diocese of Kumasi in Ghana, an initiative called "Triangle of Hope." Historically, each of the three dioceses are located in places that had been directly involved in the Slave Triangle: ships carried goods from Liverpool to what is today Ghana, which were exchanged for captured Africans, who were then shipped to Virginia to be sold as slaves, and the ships were then stocked with goods from Virginia to be sold in Liverpool, when the cycle began again. The three dioceses share work that is both an act of penance, raising awareness of the ongoing legacy of slavery, and are advocates for justice and for an end to all modern slavery and human trafficking. His rendition of "Gospel Plow" continued with a second verse, a text from the Civil Rights Movement that extends the imagery of the original text to embrace the diocese's struggle for justice:

> Well, the only chains we can stand
> Are the chains between hand and hand
> Keep your eyes on the prize
> Hold on, hold on.

By using the ready-made text, Bishop Paul's improvisation linked the work of the newly ordained not only to the offices of priests in the church, but also as agents of transformation in the ongoing struggle for justice. In effect, he gave a form to the prayer from the Anglican ordinal: "May they declare your blessings to your people; may they proclaim Christ's victory over the powers of darkness, and absolve in Christ's name those who turn to him in faith; so shall a people made whole in Christ offer spiritual sacrifices acceptable to you."

The use of the ready-made in the liturgy must be more than simply imitating past examples of liturgies as well as one can. If the ready-made is so used, the liturgy is nothing more than pastiche, imitation of some prior period of the church's life in liturgy that no longer relates to the lived reality of the faithful. Such use of the ready-made is nothing more than nostalgia or novelty and does not work for the sake of transformation of God's people. Improvisation must always attend to the deep connection between the liturgical moment and the larger world in which that moment is performed.

Improvisation in the liturgy, particularly as it relates to the ready-made, must draw deeply from the lived experience of the presider. The presider's inner life, that which propels her or him forward in both personal spirituality and vocational competence, is what matters. Improvisation requires spiritual maturity, being able to live peacefully in an ever-changing world. Such maturity makes possible improvisation that has the power to inspire the assembly in its prayer since it will come from the presider's authentic self, reflecting on the world of experience that informs his or her imagination. It is from this vantage point that the ready-made may invite transcendence. Improvisation is always a part of the deep, experiential world. The improviser "listens" to the world that is and responds to that world in his or her own work of liturgical leadership.

Sharing the Joy of Improvisation

Mark Pritchard has been a member of St. Gregory's for more than ten years, but he has been in the congregation's orbit much longer. He came to St. Gregory's through his friendship with my friend and former colleague Sara Miles. "He had a mohawk when I first met him on Street Patrol in the Castro," Sara explained when she introduced us. Raised in a suburban Lutheran congregation outside of Houston, Texas, Mark had to leave behind much of his understanding of Christianity in order to become a follower of Christ. Before he started attending on Sunday mornings, Mark came to our Morning Prayer service. Every Monday through Friday, one or two or twenty people come at eight o'clock to sit in silence, chant the psalms, listen to scripture, offer prayers, and sit in more silence. It is a beautiful beginning to the day.

Morning Prayer at St. Gregory's is based on the service found in the Book of Common Prayer, but has a few important variations. It adds seasonal variations, like singing the seven

"O Antiphons" during Advent and several resurrection troparia during the season of Easter. What visitors most frequently note is that the entire service is chanted. About half of the time, the gospel reading is chanted as well. But the greatest amount of chant is used for our communal singing of the psalter. As with many intentional communities, St. Gregory's Morning Prayer service chants between four and seven psalms for about fifteen minutes of the service. We take an ordo for the psalms designed by one of our founders, Rick Fabian. He divided the psalms into five thematic groups: Wisdom and Commandments, God's Bounty, Sin and Forgiveness, Suffering and Salvation, Peril and Rescue.

There is no set tone for chanting the psalms; each person who leads makes up their own chant tone. We find that chanting the psalms together makes it possible for us to listen more carefully to the other voices around us. We also find that improvising the psalm tone focuses our attention on the text of the psalms. Mark Pritchard says of this practice, "One thing that attending and leading Morning Prayer has taught me is that singing involves much more of the body than merely reading, or reciting from memory, aloud. I am breathing and thinking about vocal quality and other aspects of singing. It's difficult to be unengaged when you're singing."

Mark is an excellent improvisor of psalm tones. And his improvisation is almost completely based in ready-made tunes that he has picked up over the years. These aren't slavish imitations of other's work; it would be hard to identify precisely why the psalm tone he is leading sounds so familiar. The psalm tones that he improvises just sound right. Mark says of improvising psalm tones, "There are a lot of the psalms and of psalm-style chanting in the work of Bob Dylan. Consider, for example, "It's All Over Now, Baby Blue." The song is more chanted than sung. Realizing this, I experimented with using the chant-melody of the Dylan song as a psalm tone, and it works." The tune of the Dylan song is beautiful, but sad—a perfect sound to accompany the bitter and not too sweet lyrics that he wrote. But the tune bends easily and recognizably into a psalm tone, evoking both longing and pain, sadness and triumph. As a ready-made, it is almost irresistible as an improvised psalm tone.

Mark is not a trained musician. He wrote to me about his inspiration in the Dylan song: "If I had the ability to mark a music score, I could transcribe it like a psalm tone, or series of psalm tones, but if you listen to it, you'll understand what I mean." The risk that he takes as an improviser is to recognize both his strength as a liturgical leader and his technical weakness. As an improviser, he doesn't let his weakness stop his exploration. Mark told me about his desire to explore improvisation. Of his experience with the Dylan song, he wrote: "This emboldened me to use other themes from pop music to sing psalms or to sing the gospel—the tone I have come to commonly use to sing the gospel comes from the cello line that is heard during the intro of 'Strawberry Fields Forever.'" Since he told me this, I can hear the Beatles in his chanting of the gospel.

The common thread connecting improvisers is the pleasure that comes from engaging tradition with joy. Les Carpenter says, "Laughter is what brings you close to the love of God and neighbor." They also share in a cardinal rule of improvisors: you can't just think about innovation, you have to do something. Mark says of his experience of Morning Prayer at St. Gregory's, "Almost anything can be sung. That is a powerful realization for anyone whose desire is to invigorate worship. And it makes me want to go up to the bored priest saying Morning Prayer at some church and ask, 'Can't we try singing this, it will go so much better.'" When it comes to improvisation, you just have to do it—and hold it lightly.

At the conclusion of the ordination service at Liverpool Cathedral, I went down to the basement to take off my borrowed vestments. I thanked the priest who had been my handler during the service and went upstairs into the vast space of the cathedral. There were people everywhere taking pictures and sharing congratulations. I saw one of the newly ordained priests, still wearing his vestments, holding his eighteen-month-old son, nuzzling him and smiling. More than any single image from the day, it was that one that sticks with me: the image of intimacy and love shared in the midst of a grandiose building and an essentially conservative liturgy. A little later, I found Bishop Paul still wearing his golden cope and miter. "What did you think?" he asked. "All I can say is that this is a place so full of love. It was the most beautiful thing I've ever seen." That is the power of improvisation in the liturgy: it invites us to look at what we have always known and see it again, for the first time.

———————

This is what I'm learning about improvisation and liturgy . . .

Improvisation requires experience and freedom.

Improvisation takes spontaneity and reflection.

Improvisation risks what we know and asks what we long to know.

Improvisation is physical and relational.

Improvisation creates something new within and between people.

Where have you seen improvisation in a worship service, and how did it make you feel in the moment?

CHAPTER 3

Time, Energy, and Liturgy

Planning the Liturgy with Flexibility

Improvisation is a practice that can disrupt and remake the liturgy in a way that invites transformation. And, if the liturgy is for anything, other than giving glory to God, it is to transform us. But the energy of improvisation has to be rooted and grounded in community, tradition, and practice; otherwise, it quickly devolves into novelty and more quickly becomes tiresome. Authentic improvisation cannot be practiced apart from planning, and this requires liturgical leaders to attend to many different variables, including time and energy.

By time, I mean both sequential time as found in the church calendar and the meaning of time as it is defined by the readings appointed for days and seasons. For example, the way that, just as we are ending the season of Pentecost and preparing for the season of Advent, we hear readings that lean into judgment and the end of things.

By energy, I mean the flow of affection, connection, discovery, and beauty that work for the sake of our transformation. For example, there is an uptick in people's affect when the liturgy shifts from the people's prayers to the exchange of Christ's Peace. As we consider these variables, it's essential to look at how we plan liturgy, particularly how we think about our planning in relation to the overall mission and ministry of the church. I begin with the assumption that all planning is provisional. Let me explain what I mean.

I was raised in a home designed and built in 1964 by an architect named Ursula Oppenheimer. I remember her a little; in my memories, she always has on a tweed suit and a serious expression. And, as her name suggests, she was German, which made her seem exotic to me, a boy living in suburban Houston, Texas. But more than remembering her, I remember her work. Specifically, I think of the blueprints she drew of our house. She left a set with us after we moved into the house in 1965. As a child, I was fascinated by these plans, the huge sheets of paper with that distinct smell and feel that came from the photosensitive ferric compound by which they were made. I would get the plans off of the top shelf in my father's closet and unroll them on the dining room table and look at the hidden bones of our house. There was something uncanny about sitting in the house described by the blueprints, looking around, and seeing how the walls fit together, thinking about where the hidden electric and plumbing supplies had been tucked in, wondering how the upstairs of the house and the downstairs fit together. Seeing these strange details made me think that I knew more about the secret life of the house than people who just happened to drive by and look at it, or walk inside to pay a visit. I was also struck by the differences between Ursula Oppenheimer's blueprints and the house that I inhabited.

Like most blueprints, the design and the actual house built from the plan weren't the same precisely. Instead of a den with a tall, cathedral ceiling and a balcony at the top of the stairs overlooking the whole thing, there was a bedroom upstairs; my mother became pregnant with my younger sister soon after the plans were completed—so an extra bedroom was tucked into that space. The plans called for very on-trend, 1960s, marbleized, white, composite tiles downstairs, but it was executed in wood parquet instead. There was supposed to be a raised brick planter in front of the house, but it wasn't there either; something about our neighborhood building code prevented it. There were other alterations as well. Even though our house wasn't precisely built as planned, you could tell that the house came from the plans. The blueprint represented the house that Ursula Oppenheimer saw in her imagination. And the house my parents built from her design was different. The blueprints were essential, but the house was not the same as the blueprints.

When it comes to planning the liturgy, the very same needs to be said about the prayer book. Just like a blueprint, the prayer book gives us precise instructions for how to build the daily and weekly services of the church. Just like a blueprint, the prayer book includes all sorts of information for worship that is more or less invisible to the average worshiper; I'm thinking of the rubrics and all the sections entitled "About the Service."

It's worth remembering that there are two categories of rubrics: permissive and prescriptive. Permissive rubrics describe actions that the presider and people *may* do liturgically. Prescriptive rubrics are more like orders; you *have to* do the liturgical act in a certain way. In the Celebration and Blessing of a Marriage, those to be married *may* enter accompanied by "a hymn, psalm, or anthem,"[1] but at the exchange of vows, the couple *has to* join hands.[2]

The distinction between these two kinds of rubrics isn't always explicit. The reason music at the entrance is optional but joining hands is not isn't stated in the rubric. Because of this, it is valuable to be curious about rubrics and their purpose, as we choose to follow them. Some rubrics are like the instructions for assembling Ikea furniture: you disobey them at your peril. And like those inscrutable instructions for putting together a good, cheap bookcase, the more times you examine the rubrics, the more intuitive they become. A good way to learn from the rubrics is to be curious about them, ask them what they intend, and read them with a generous spirit—as well as with an eye on history and scholarship.

The liturgies in which God's people participate don't always go according to the plan laid out in the prayer book. More often than not, if you lay the prayer book next to the printed worship leaflet, you will see the differences that can be made when it comes to planning the liturgy. All of which is to say, liturgical planners are hackers; everyone practices the art of disruption.

---

1. Book of Common Prayer, 423.
2. Ibid., 427.

Many things invite us to disrupt the liturgies we plan. Things like pastoral events in the life of a congregation, liturgical leaders forgetting to show up for the service, the cycles of nature, the too frequent civil crises and heartaches, and a thousand other unexpected events that can catch us by surprise have to be considered in planning.

On Christmas Day in 2016, the last Sunday of the year, we decided to alter the plan of the liturgy. Because of the fall's election, for many of us it was a time marked by anxiety. Of these many fears, we worried that the legality of same-sex marriage might be undone. So on Christmas Day, after the Liturgy of the Word and before the Liturgy of the Table, I officiated at the marriage of two women. Although they had planned on a wedding sometime in the next few weeks, had their marriage license, and had received their pastoral instruction for marriage, the three of us decided to have a wedding minutes before the service began.

Just as the exchange of the Peace was ending, I said, "I want to let you all know that we're going to do something a little different today. We are going to bear witness to the marriage of Kerri and Jen." There was a gasp. One woman began to weep. Amid so much fear of the unknown, because so many variables seemed beyond our control, despite other plans that were being made, we decided it was time to alter our plans. The pastoral necessity was clear to us, even though the prayer book didn't quite know what we were doing. At any moment, you may get a text, or get caught in a downpour, or read the front page of the paper and think, "The plans that I have made are just not going to work. We must begin again."

Since the work of planning the liturgy always includes hacking the prayer book, an essential practice to bring to planning the liturgy is flexibility: being flexible to what we do not know. It is far too easy to stay stuck in our plans. When that happens, it is easy for the liturgy to become a museum piece and not a living thing. Flexibility, like improvisation, is a practice. It is not the same thing as just doing anything you please. Flexibility in planning means paying attention to what may seem peripheral, unnecessary, inconvenient, or uncomfortable. This requires a willingness to engage compassion and curiosity in planning.

Flexibility does not mean that we get to toss the prayer book out the window; the blueprint is always valuable, even when we have to adjust it to the circumstances in which we are living. The value of the plan will always remain. Whether we follow the service word for word from the prayer book, or if we decide to hack the book to make a new kind of liturgy, embracing flexibility means honoring the intention and spirit of the text. And just as I did in my boyhood wondering of the blueprints of my family home, we have to pay attention to the not always obvious way that things fit together in the liturgy. When we practice flexibility in planning the liturgy, we get to examine the arrangement of words and action, how the music and silence relate to each other, how stillness and motion must fit together in a harmonious whole. The choices we make in planning the liturgy must pay attention to the blueprint provided in the prayer book.

Flexibility is a founding principle of St. Gregory's. The congregation first worshipped together in 1978, and Bishop William Swing both encouraged and allowed us to be intentionally experimental in planning the liturgy. This allowance has been made manifest in many different forms over the years. For example, our baptismal liturgy places the covenant after the candidates are bathed at the font. The affirmation of the covenant is one in which all present are called to participate, not only the ones who are newly baptized. So we invite the whole congregation to affirm the faith of the church while the water and oil are still flowing off the newly baptized.

In part, we do this to shift the focus from our agency in baptism to what God is doing. There is no sense of a *quid pro quo* between God and us; it is God who is at work, making us a new creation in baptism. We show up in our imperfection and beauty in the confidence that God's promise is stronger than the words that we mortals repeat. We sequence our baptismal liturgy in this way because the entire liturgy of baptism is the covenant that we make with God and that God makes with us. Claiming flexibility as a core value in planning liturgy makes it possible for us to experiment with the gifts we have received in the liturgy, discovering new ways of praising God for her infinite goodness and generosity toward us.

There is no such thing as a perfect liturgy. The only perfect liturgy is the one taking place eternally in God's heavenly presence, so strangely described in John's Revelation. Every other liturgy is working with a set of blueprints and adapting them to the tasks at hand: the pastoral imperatives of the community, the building in which the liturgy is performed, the cultural settings within which the liturgy is planned, the individuals whom we hope to draw in by the liturgy, and many other considerations. At its best, the work we do in planning the liturgy is the art of disruption.

Clock Time and Heart Time

One aspect of planning liturgy is time. There are two senses of time that we have received in Christian tradition: *chronos* and *kairos*. *Chronos* refers to sequential time, one moment following another, one moment being influenced by another. *Kairos* refers to time that is opportune, meaningful, and full of God's promise. *Chronos* is about quantitative data. *Kairos* is about qualitative data. *Chronos* is clock time. *Kairos* is heart time. We must attend to both of these senses of time in the liturgy.

Both *chronos* and *kairos* relate to the metaphor of the blueprint. *Chronos* is the part of the blueprint that tells how the house will fit together and withstand the natural forces around it, including the physical limitations that influence the design. *Kairos* is the part of the blueprint that tells the deeper story of the family that will occupy the space, their hopes, dreams, desires, and the accidents that influence the design.

Chronos in the liturgy matters for practical reasons. If there is no posted time for the service, then nobody will come, or if there is no idea of how long the service will run, people may get up and leave before it's over. At St. Gregory's, we discovered something about chronos-time that has changed the way we invite families and children into the liturgy.

Like many Episcopal churches, St. Gregory's has two morning services, one at 8:00 and the other at 11:00. The early service was added to our schedule in the late 1980s after we had purchased the property where our church building now stands. Before this time, we had been meeting in a rented side chapel at Trinity (now Trinity–St. Peter's) Episcopal Church in the middle of San Francisco. This temporary home welcomed us for seventeen years. When it became clear to us that our congregation was not only a viable community but one that was growing and thriving, we raised enough money to purchase property in the Potrero Hill neighborhood of San Francisco. At that time it was a mixed industrial and residential neighborhood; homes were up the hill, and small manufacturers were at the bottom of the hill. Our property was at the bottom, on an old gravel quarry that had been carved from the side of the hill. There was a house on the corner, built in the 1940s, and a machine shop next to it. The house was renovated and became the parish office and classroom building.

Because we wanted to be present in the neighborhood before we had the funds in hand to build our church building, we renovated the upstairs of the house into a chapel. It was a long, narrow space that we arranged with the altar table near the entrance door and the lectern opposite it at the other end of the room. Chairs were set up facing each other between these two spaces. It was a small worship space, but it was enough for us to host our new neighbors. Because the primary service would continue on Sunday morning at Trinity at 10:00, we scheduled the service in the neighborhood for 8:00. The two rectors would preach and preside at St. Gregory's on Potrero Hill, and then would dash across town to St. Gregory's at Trinity. The Potrero Hill congregation began to grow. We had plastered the neighborhood with notices: "Do you like to sing and dance? Join us at 8:00 at the corner of Mariposa and De Haro Street."

Six years later our church building was completed and consecrated. Before the first service in the new church, members met at Trinity and packed up the liturgical materials we had acquired over our seventeen years in residence, and we moved across town. The plan had been to have a single Sunday morning liturgy, but the early service had been so meaningful to our neighbors that it continued.

It was a small service. There was no choir. Although the DNA of our main liturgy was evident in the early service, there were differences. The later service grew larger and larger; the early service topped out at around twenty-five attendees. It was a quieter service, less complicated and shorter in time than the late service. Many members who came to the late service had never been to the early service, and vice versa. For the first thirteen years in our new home, the early service became, like so many early services in Episcopal churches, the "low mass." And then something happened; we were surprised by chronos-time.

It started little by little. First, Mateo and Virginia came to the early service with their young children. Then another family with young children came. Although there had been a very brief children's program during the early service, it was discontinued around 2008, mainly because more families wanted their children with them in church. I also wanted to have children present for the entire service. If we really believe that our liturgy is about formation, then having children present is the only correct choice; I just didn't think it would be at the early service. More and more families with children began to come to the early service. One morning I asked a young mother why they went to the quiet, early service and not to the later one. "My kids are up every morning at 6:30," she said. "There's no way we're going to make it to a service that begins at 10:00 or 11:00 on a Sunday morning. By then, my youngest is going down for her morning nap."

We had assumed that our 8:00 service would continue as it always had: a liturgy for adults who wanted a quiet time in the morning. Until they began to join us, it never occurred to me that it might be a time for families. This was a clear example of the church's understanding of chronos-time coming into conflict with the chronos-time of people's lives. In the back of my head

I kept hearing a voice that said, "Every Episcopal church has a quiet morning service." As more and more children came with their families to our early service, that voice mattered less and less.

There was conflict when children started coming to the early service. Children communicate on their own terms, expressing their pleasure or boredom openly and sometimes loudly. Adults do likewise, but their expressions of pleasure or boredom are usually more contained. One particular Sunday, a new family's children were active and noisy throughout the early service. Afterward, a member who had started attending the service a couple of years before came up to me in tears. "This used to be a wonderful respite for me, and these kids are just too much." She left and never came back. Her sense of chronos-time and the congregation's didn't match. I was very sorry when she left. Her life as a public school teacher was always stressful, and the congregation had become a support for her, but the logic of families with young children coming to the early service was undeniable to me.

The transformation of the early service at St. Gregory's from a quiet to a lively time has significantly changed the way we approach worship. Instead of it being an adults-only service, it is now our main family service. When visitors with children come to the later service, I encourage them to go to the earlier one. If they have some experience of the Episcopal Church and the way that early services are typically kept low key and quiet, they usually express surprise. "I never imagined coming to an 8:00 service with my kids—but it would work out so much better for us." Instead of a congregation of twenty-five adults, the early service now welcomes between forty and sixty people, with fifteen to twenty of those being children under twelve years old.

But what about those who miss the way things have always been? I can answer that question by turning to the idea of kairos-time.

Kairos-time in the liturgy matters for soulish reasons: if there is no meaning to the time we spend together, no time to connect our lives one to another and God, people may confuse the liturgy with a clubby gathering of friends or a political action committee. Each moment of the liturgy has to fit together in the same way that the parts of a house fit together, or else the whole thing will collapse.

Whenever we change the structure of the liturgy, whenever we plan some innovation, it will result in loss and possibly conflict. However, if we consider kairos-time in planning the liturgy, it is easier to talk about change as a part of the larger meaning of the community. The change in St. Gregory's early service, initially caused by considerations of chronos-time, was also an invitation for us to consider the liturgy in kairos-time. Our mission statement says, "St. Gregory's Church invites people to see God's image in all humankind, to sing and dance to Jesus's lead, and to become God's friends." The fullness of time that *kairos* indicates is time that includes all people, even children. This fullness of time also means that we must actively seek God's image in the lives of all people, even children. The friendship into which Jesus invites his disciples is for all people, even children.

When children became a significant part of our early service, we had to recognize that the Holy Spirit was offering us a gift: a new way to understand our mission. This gift was a kairos-gift; the fullness of time was all around us, and we just had to respond to it. As the congregation's leader, I was able to speak to the conflict by saying that the changes in the early service meant we were living faithfully into our mission. Instead of disrupting the liturgy for no good reason, we changed our plans in response to the gift that God was and had always been giving to us.

As time passed, I noticed two ways in which kairos-time was changing our community. As we lived into the gift of having children in the early service, two prayer book hacks have transformed St. Gregory's.

Many people who had attended the early service when it was a smaller, quieter service missed the sense of meditative stillness we had enjoyed. Children's presence in the service was enlivening, but there were fewer moments of extended silence in the early service. Olivia, a longtime member who had been involved in a Taizé service some years before, was one such person. "I really am glad that the kids are here, but I miss the silence." We wondered together how we might add intentional time for silence, psalm-chanting, and *lectio divina* into Sunday mornings. We decided to plan an additional thirty minutes of the early service that would come before the main eucharistic liturgy. I decided to hack a liturgy from the Eastern Christian tradition and planned a service called "Daybreak"—one way of translating the Byzantine liturgical word *Orthros*.

The service begins with the same morning song every Sunday, Psalm 19, as we offer incense. We sing a text from the *Orthodox trisagion* prayers, "Come heavenly comforter." We chant between three and five psalms, using a tone that the volunteer cantor teaches by ear; Olivia is one of these cantors. Following psalm chanting, there is a period of silence, a time for each person to rest in the gift of the Holy Spirit. There is one reading, followed by another full five minutes of silence. As this time of chant and silence continues, people arrive for the eucharistic liturgy and find a seat. Daybreak concludes by singing a hymn, which leads the congregation into the entrance rite of the eucharist.

St. Gregory's disrupts both the prayer book and our own liturgical customs. If we sense a need for some additional piece of ritual action, we recognize the provisional quality of the liturgy and use our freedom to make a change. Disrupting our own liturgy frees us from idolizing our practice. This is not because we don't care about what we've done in the past; we care deeply about our practice.

As in many churches, we spend a lot of time planning and a lot of time reviewing what happens in Sunday liturgies. Recognizing the provisional nature of our liturgy is a part of this planning and review. Each week we look at the previous Sunday's worship; we talk about what we saw, what was surprising, what was boring—and what we should plan to do differently in the coming week's liturgy. In doing this, we're not trying to get our liturgy "right" as much as to understand what's happening among us as we worship together. More and more, I see that the practice of looking back and looking forward in the church can, if we're not attentive to Jesus's invitation to transformation, lead us into either nostalgia for some imagined perfect past or anxiety about an unknown and threatening future. Instead, our challenge is to pay attention to what God is doing among us right now—to stay prayerfully awake to what's happening.

On some Sundays, Daybreak welcomes fifteen people; on other Sundays, there may only be five people present. The number of attendees is not the main point; the consistency of our quiet opening of the day insures that those who need silence for their spiritual practice can find it with us every Sunday. A couple of people come only for Daybreak and leave before the eucharistic liturgy begins. And there are usually children present. Although they can be rambunctious later in the service, the children who are present seem to value the silence. They may sit and draw, or join in the chant.

We ring Japanese temple bells to indicate the beginning of each silence. When I introduce children to these liturgical tools, I challenge them to listen carefully to the deep resonance of the bells: "Close your eyes and see how long you can hear the bell before it stops ringing, then open your eyes." I watch the children concentrate on the sound until the silence becomes a part of them.

Children have a distinct intelligence in the liturgy. But children are more able to engage the liturgy if they are given something to do in the service. Children are wiser than adults sometimes believe; they know if the tasks they are assigned in the service are significant. Adults can well afford to give away real work to children, and so we welcome children as full participants and leaders in the service. We welcome children as readers and liturgical leaders, as eucharistic ministers and participants in sermon sharing. This inclusion of children in the leadership of the liturgy comes from our desire to share with them in the full life of Christ's Body. This practice is not without risk. Children perform their liturgical leadership as they are, with small bodies and sometimes quiet voices. Sometimes children become bored with the service before their leadership duties are completed. One Sunday, Soren, a nine-year-old liturgical leader, took off his vestments during the peace and came to the altar in a tee-shirt and shorts. "I got too hot," he explained.

We hope that children take their liturgical work seriously. And we know that there will be times when children will behave differently from their adult colleagues in leadership. When we attend to kairos-time in the liturgy, we find that we can live through the different leadership styles and the more limited attention span of some children. We also shortened the length of the early service to be more responsive to the needs of children in chronos-time.

Paying attention to time—in both the quantitative and qualitative sense—is essential in planning the liturgy. Each sort of time contributes to the beauty of the liturgy and its transformative potential in people's lives. Successful disruption of the liturgy requires taking time into consideration. One further sort of time must be considered when we look at planning the liturgy: eschatological time.

The End of Time

Eschaton refers to ending. The ending to which eschatology points is the final ending, the end of the world, which is why it seems sort of spooky to many people. But the ending to which eschatology points is always the ending that is held in God's loving hands; it is the end of all things, but also the beginning of all things. The violent mythology that sometimes surrounds religious talk about the end of the world shouldn't put us off: that is a human construction.

Paying attention to eschatological time invites us to consider the Sunday service as a part of an eternal reality, a single moment in which Christ is all and in all. Eschatological time reminds us that in the liturgy, we join Jesus Christ as he tramples down the system of oppression and violence that swirls around us. As we attend to eschatological time, the liturgy opens our eyes to see a peaceful alternative to everything that oppresses God's creation. And, as our eyes are open to this world, we come to know

God more clearly as love. As we share the liturgy with our vision focused on God's future, we may change our orientation toward God, seeing God as the one who calls us to new life. Or, as we sometimes perform this reality in the liturgy, we turn to repentance. In the liturgy, we turn to a new way of knowing God, being changed by God's love, and going forth to change the world.

In December 1998, during the church's eschatological season of Advent, I was invited to imagine violence and embrace vengeance or practice forgiveness and release. The experience was a profound lesson about the end of things.

I have always painted. Although today I practice icon painting, there was a period when I painted landscapes. At the time, I lived in a house that had a studio behind it where I would paint. At the time of this incident, I was painting a landscape for my sister. I left town to lead a retreat one weekend, and when I returned late on a Saturday night, I found that someone had broken into my studio. I walked in through the open door and turned on the lights. Things were in disarray, stuff all over the floor, and the painting that I'd been working on was on its easel. Whoever broke in had taken the time to open a jar of bright orange acrylic and painted a big "X" over the canvas. I didn't mind so much that the thief had taken a camera and some other things. I was wrecked by the fact that the thief had taken the time to paint an "X" over a painting I'd been working on. Since I had to be at an early liturgy the next day at the cathedral where I worked, I turned off the lights, secured the door, went into my house, and drifted into an anxious sleep.

The next day, the third Sunday of Advent, I sat through three liturgies and three times heard the words of the Prophet Isaiah: "Be strong, do not fear! Here is your God. He will come with vengeance, with terrible recompense. He will come and save you" (Isaiah 35:4). Each time that I heard it, I thought about the ruined painting in my studio. "That sounds about right," I said to myself. "Bring it on." I imagined that my anger was the occasion for God's vengeance to be visited on whoever broke into my studio and ruined my painting. As each of the liturgies progressed, I sunk deeper into my anger and hunger for vengeance.

After church that day, when I returned from serving in three liturgies, I went into the studio to clean things up. I arranged the stuff that had been disarrayed and cleared up the mess on the floor. I put broken glass in the trashcan and repaired the broken lock on the door. Then I turned to look at the ruined painting on its easel. I looked at the soft greens and blues of the landscape with the bright, almost neon orange "X" painted on it by some unknown adversary. I decided to leave the vandalized painting on the easel. I kept it there for months. Every time that I'd go into the studio, I would look at it and wonder why it had been ruined.

At first there was nothing but anger. Then the anger changed into sadness. I put away my brushes and my paints, having lost my interest in painting, and would just look at the painting that had been ruined. I'd wonder about its ending and about the world in which a random act of vandalism can make such a lasting impression. It seemed I needed to keep the painting near me to keep kindled my desire for vengeance. I kept it in view because I needed to bear witness to the violent act. Eventually I realized that I didn't really want revenge on the thief who had ruined it—I didn't really want the vandal to be punished. That didn't make sense to me. What I really wanted was healing for a world in which violence and anger sometimes seem to be the most powerful thing. The answer to my passion wasn't vengeance; it was something more rooted in my soul. The answer to my anger was releasing the unknown other to God's love. Eventually, I did the sensible thing and threw the painting in the trash.

Because eschatological time has been so burdened with violent imagery for so long, we have to be clear about the ways we attend to violence in relation to the liturgy. When it comes to planning liturgy, we must remember that the revelation of Christ means that God is free of vengeance. We can no longer plan liturgy that winks at retribution and violence; the time for that is passed as we live into the culture of God's love. It can be hard to practice this in planning and performing the liturgy. For as long as we have stood in the blood of the slain victim in our midst, relishing in its redness and glistening power to satisfy us, we have believed that our violent imaginations were simply a reflection of God's desire. But the liturgy must show us that the God of Jesus Christ is different from our idolatry of God because that idolatry will always contain violence.

When we consider eschatological time in the liturgy, we hold in our hearts the truth that God does not love you and hate those whom you hate, or that God is on your side and against your enemy. God makes no distinction between worthy and unworthy: all of us need both deliverance from our lust for vengeance and God's blessing of peace. When we plan the liturgy, we must remember that God is raining mercy on us continually. Too often, we cover ourselves with parasols of denial, even as we are drenched in the same blessing as our enemies. Peace, love, blessing, and mercy are truths of eschatological time that must always be reflected in the liturgy. Because of our eschatology of peace, the prayers of the people at St. Gregory's always include the petitions, "For those we have wronged, for our enemies and all who wrong us" and "For forgiveness, generosity, and love among all people everywhere, and for the coming kingdom of peace."

Throughout the gospel narrative, the time that matters most to Jesus is always the end of time. Jesus fully expected his generation would see the end of things as they had ever been. If you imagine that this means a big apocalypse—an action-packed, asteroid-colliding, adrenaline-fueled catastrophe—it seems that those who wrote us the story of Jesus were wrong. But if we listen to the conversation God is having with the universe, we can get a sense of the point Jesus is making: the end has come, and we stand as witnesses to the beginning of the new age.

Jesus taught that everything deflecting us from the glory of God was ending. Jesus taught that God was active on the fringes of society. He taught that the status quo was passing away and would be replaced by a new relationship between God and all people: nothing could be the same, not even the ways people had always known God. Jesus proclaimed a new order based on God's self-giving love and our imitation of that love. This must always be reflected in the liturgy.

When we entertain vengeance as an option in the liturgy, we miss the power of eschatological time in the liturgy, which is always present in the liturgy. Maybe the most familiar is the eucharistic acclamation, "Christ has died, Christ is risen, Christ will come again." That well-worn trope rehearses the simple truth that Christ's coming is always accompanied by endings, the end of things as they've always been. I sometimes wonder if it would not be better to locate the eschaton not in some distant future beyond imagining, but in the everyday endings of our lives. Paintings are vandalized, and loved ones die in God's peace every day. It might be more powerful to say, "Christ has died, Christ is risen, Christ comes again."

I don't have any trouble believing in the end of things. Endings happen every day. What begins in security can end in tragedy. What starts with hope can be turned upside down by random chance. Endings are familiar. And the eschatological ending of things is a good place from which to begin to conceive the shape of the liturgy.

Channeling Energy in the Liturgy

There is a flow of energy in every social gathering, including the assembly of the church for worship. Every liturgy contains moments that are relatively low energy: listening to the reading of scripture or moments of silence in the intercessions. Even the gathering of the assembly may be a time of low energy, particularly if the intention of the liturgy's planners is for people to keep holy silence when they enter the church building. Likewise, every liturgy contains moments of high energy: singing a well-known, rollicking hymn or an extended period of sharing the Peace. Many people consider that the breaking of the bread in the Great Thanksgiving is the highest of high points of energy. Over the years, at St. Gregory's, we have designed the moment of highest energy in the liturgy to be the dismissal, which for us invariably is "Let us bless the Lord," with the response "Thanks be to God."

The dismissal in the 1979 prayer book is itself a hack of earlier prayer books; you won't find it in any of the first three prayer books of the Episcopal Church. It's not even a required part of the liturgy in the Rite One service in the current prayer book. The earlier prayer books simply ended the service with the priest blessing the people. There was nothing else to indicate that it was time to get going, no indication that the liturgy was to move on from the church to the everyday reality of people's lives.

Instead, in earlier prayer books, there was a more privatized idea of the liturgy. People came to church to have their own time with God, and that was that. The dismissal as a prayer book hack in the 1979 Book of Common Prayer was an attempt to reclaim earlier practice in the life of the church, going all the way back to the fourth century and the customs of liturgy then. Those early dismissals were imitative of the ways that formal civic gatherings would end in the Roman world. The formality of the dismissal was not far off from the bartender at closing time saying, "You don't have to go home, but you have to go."

The dismissal is the high point of energy in the liturgy at St. Gregory's because we want our people to experience action in the world as continuous with their work in the liturgy. We want people to talk to each other, to reflect with each other, to share coffee and snacks with each other. We want people to make the connection between their everyday lives and their shared lives in the liturgy, and so we put the coffee pots on the altar table. The sacrament of the table doesn't end with the dismissal, but it does shift focus.

At the dismissal, the sacramental energy becomes more intentionally relational, and there are tasks we attend to for the sake of this intentionality. We have to welcome visitors, engaging them in conversation about their experience of the service or what brought them through our doors. We have to make pastoral connections with people, particularly those who may have shared difficult chapters in their lives through prayer or sermon sharing. The liturgical leaders have to connect with each other about what they noticed in the liturgy and what might need to change. The energy of the dismissal gives us the boost we need to continue the feasting. We begin planning the liturgy with this energetic ending in mind.

The energy of worship must move in a direction if the liturgy is going to be lively. The flow of energy in the liturgy is always toward the congregation's movement out into the world. This is because the place where we will most assuredly meet God is outside the doors of the church. We may gather inside the church to strengthen ourselves, but we can never hide in the church; hiding keeps us from doing the work of the gospel. God desires that we be fully human, that we become more fully human. And becoming more fully human happens when we leave the liturgy revived and ready to seek God in the lives of those whom we encounter. The energy of the liturgy must move in this particular direction. God desires that we live in the absolute truth of ourselves, which is peace between God and us and each other. It is the energy of this peacemaking that must be woven into our plans for the liturgy.

Becoming fully human is living into God's desire—and, paradoxically, it is the only way that we can ever hope to become as God is. To be like God is to be fully human. Not perfect. Not sinless. But more and more becoming free from our feeble attempts at impressing God with our piety. Becoming less interested in the ways that we can hide our shame and always appear to be right. Growing less addicted to the cry of our ego and more open to the fullness of God's Spirit within us. The mystery of God's love is in us, in our fulsome, beautiful humanity. The energy that is generated in this revelation is one that drives the liturgy forward in joy.

The Energy of Joy and Freedom

The flow of energy must always move in the direction of joy. The feeling of joy is much more than that of contentment or happiness. Joy is the fullness of that sense of congruity with God that is often called prayer. It is the feeling I get in the morning when I anticipate a day of painting. I feel exhilarated—it is alight with joy. This is what the church's liturgy needs to be.

One way to attend to the movement of energy toward joy is simply to reflect on where you know joy in your life. As with everything centered on God, it will most likely be in the everyday stuff wherein you spend your time. Or it may be in those exceptional moments when you step out of the ordinary into something more. My experience tells me that joy is most often incarnate; joy and bodies just go together. Maybe joy is in your body when you go for a run or a walk. Perhaps joy is in your body when you dance or sing. Maybe joy is in your body when, like me, your hands are at work making beauty. All of these experiences are just another way of talking about prayer. Too often I've thought of prayer in the same way I've thought of self-improvement; it's something that I have to do in order to be a better person. And every time that I think of prayer in these terms, the joy just drains away. There is a scandalous impracticality to prayer—just as there is with joy.

What blocks the energy of the liturgy moving toward joy is the frustrating experience of not knowing how to get to where I want to be. It's like the time that I tried to build a harpsichord. I had the desire, I even had some of the skills, but I didn't have the time or the energy or the real expertise to take on such a challenging project. In planning the liturgy, we have to give up on any sort of unattainable outcome and show up to the task with a consideration of what we can accomplish.

More than thirty years ago, I was responsible for planning and leading a diocesan-wide youth eucharist at Christ Church Cathedral in Houston, Texas. Instead of replaying a summer camp-style youth service, I had something else in mind. A few years before, I had been deeply moved by the liturgy at a retreat led by some of the brothers from the Taizé community in France. It had made such an impression on me that I thought I could borrow bits and pieces of it and roll them into the youth eucharist. When I talked to the organist at the cathedral about it, a hugely talented and very classically minded man, he just sort of gave me a blank stare. "Don't worry," I quickly said, "I can take care of the Taizé piece." This was some years before this kind of music was well used in that diocese; it was little wonder that I got the blank stare from my colleague.

The problem was that I didn't really have the musical ability to make it work. I knew that the final effect should be one of the solo voices and instruments gradually growing in a beautiful crescendo of sound, but I had no idea how to weave all the instruments and pieces together. I said to the youth singers and musicians who gathered on the Sunday afternoon of the service, "Don't worry, just kind of start soft and get louder—and we'll throw the trumpet in at the end." To say that my enthusiasm blinded me to the technical difficulty of the task would be a colossal understatement. Needless to say, it was not a shining moment of liturgical transformation. In fact, it was just a mess. The energy that should have flowed freely through the service—the same energy I experienced with the youth doing liturgy at summer camp—was replaced by a weird, ersatz kind of Taizé service that satisfied no one. Sticking with forms that were known and loved, not overreaching, would have been a better path forward.

When planning the liturgy begins to feel daunting, loosen your grip on your desire for what you think is perfect, and focus your love on what is good enough. The movement of energy toward joy has much more to do with just showing up than any imagined finished product. When we plan the liturgy, we must rely on the energy of God to continually kindle in us the warmth of divine light. We must turn away from the false promises of the ego and turn toward the generosity of God at work in us, keeping joy alive.

The flow of energy in the liturgy must always move toward freedom. Our freedom comes when we recognize that we are freed by the limits placed on us by our relationships—to each other and to God. Freedom comes when we let go of our fear of death and allow what needs to die in us die. Freedom comes when we let go of the limitless possibilities that keep us frozen in life and choose to walk the path before us. Freedom comes when we let go of our need to control the other person and simply love the other person. Freedom comes when we give up on our need to have everything and simply have what gives us life. Freedom comes when we care less for being perfect than we do about being real. As the Book of Common Prayer says:

> O God, who art the author of peace and lover of concord, in knowledge of whom standeth our eternal life, whose service is perfect freedom: Defend us, thy humble servants, in all assaults of our enemies; that we, surely trusting in thy defense, may not fear the power of any adversaries; through the might of Jesus Christ our Lord. *Amen.*[3]

Every Easter, for as long as I have served at St. Gregory's, we have sung Ben Allaway's powerful song, "Freedom Come." Ben wrote it as a call and response song. Beneath the lyrics are the people's rhythmic phrase "freedom come." It is an insistent phrase, not politely asking God to bring us liberation, but asking in the voice of a child who wants more chocolate milk before dinner. The God who promises us freedom is as good as her word, and so we cry out over and over, "freedom come." The verses that float over this refrain are similarly demanding and full of confidence in God's power:

> Inside these walls, freedom come, freedom come.
> Come one and all, freedom come, freedom come.
> Come for the healing; we will pray for the healing.
> Come for the victory; we will share the victory.
> Come with your burden: we will share your burden.
> Come with your sorrow; we will share your sorrow.
> Come if you're guilty; we are all guilty.
> Come with forgiveness; we all need forgiveness.
> Bring your anger. Sing it away.
> Bring your hatred. Sing it away.
> Bring your burden. Pray it away.
> Bring your sorrow. Pray it away.
> Hallelujah. O Jesus, come.
> O freedom, come. Hallelujah.[4]

---

3. Book of Common Prayer, 57.
4. Ben Allaway, "Freedom Come" (Santa Barbara, CA: Santa Barbara Music, 1996).

As we sing these words, the energy of each phrase intensifying, the meaning of each word sinking more profoundly into our souls, the power of life over death is made real. As we sing, I look out at the faces of the people, candlelit in the brightness of our Easter Vigil. I see those whose loved ones have died, those who have suffered sickness, those who are unemployed or homeless. In their faces I also see eyes aglow with the burning desire for justice, for relief, for a new chance in life.

Singing "Freedom Come" in 2020 was unlike anything we had experienced before; COVID-19 caused us to reconsider how we would use well-loved and familiar parts of the liturgy. Along with our music director, I had been making plans for the Vigil a few weeks before the lockdown began. We had to change our plans, and as with the Good Friday liturgy, I understood that our Easter celebration would have to be one that "felt like us," and that it would have to include the music that filled us with the joy of the Resurrection.

Like all of the liturgies at that time, the Vigil was livestreamed from participants' homes. Twenty-seven people shared in leading the service, including groups of people in different households. The liturgy began in the darkness, people lighting their individual candles as Tim and Kelsey sang the *Exsultet*. Then the long series of lessons were taken by people reading in groups from their homes, dividing the speaking roles as befit the passage. The originality and playfulness of the different groups enlivened the readings.

After the third reading, Matt and Terri led us in singing "Freedom Come," the song that so perfectly captures the joy of Easter for the community. When I saw their faces on the screen, I knew it was going to be another playful, original performance. Matt sat at the piano, banging out the steady beat of the chords, singing the leader's part. Terri stood by his side and sang the people's response to these lines. And then, it happened; as she sang each of the responses, Terri held up a cue card with the words written in magic marker. I laughed out loud for the joy radiating from her. Other households led other hymns; Clark, Dina, and their two children played accordion, stand-up bass, and violin for "Mary, Don't You Weep." Joe and Abby recruited one of their housemates to form a trio singing Matthew Priest's hauntingly beautiful canticle, "Say to the Mountains."

COVID-19 shifted the energy of the Vigil, but did not diminish it. Our liturgy was not what we had planned, but it proclaimed Christ's resurrection as surely as any we had celebrated in the church building. The energy that washed over us was full of joy and hope; on every screen I saw faces that reflected what looked like freedom to me. And in the pandemic, I saw that every death and every loss that we had feared was eclipsed by the light of Christ's neverending life. The freedom that comes to us from the empty tomb resonated in our bodies even though we were separated. That energy filled us as one body in prayer. And I knew that the pandemic could not cancel Easter.

From the Perfect to the Real

A final image comes to mind when I consider the work of planning the liturgy. I have painted icons for twenty years or more, and whenever I paint an icon, the hardest thing to do is to begin. Icons are painted on a pure, smooth, white board, with no imperfections, no rough patches or mistakes. It is an entirely blank, beautiful space where anything is possible. And it stays that way until you add lines and paint. Then it loses its emptiness and becomes, sometimes, a mess. You have to work with what you have, even with the mistakes that you make. As a container, the board of an icon gives you limits. If you're doing your work well, you don't use a huge number of colors; you try and make the surface luminous with a limited palette. If you work slowly, using the little that you have, then the result is beautiful. If you overwork it, using too many colors, you end up with mud. It's hard work that takes all of your attention. And of course the easiest thing to do is not begin at all, and just keep the blank white board in storage.

So it is with planning the liturgy; the easiest part may be before you make any decisions at all. There is nothing as perfect as the prayer book sitting safely on your desk, red leather and gold embossing all aglow. But our work is not about perfection so much as it is about becoming real. Once you set yourself on the course of planning the liturgy, disrupting the prayer book in ways that bring more life, more of a meaningful sense of time, and more energy that draws the people to take up the work of Christ in the world, then you will discover transformation.

———————————

This is what I'm learning about planning liturgy . . .

Planning requires that I know the hearts of the people I lead in worship.

Planning means that the best time is the time I'm in right now.

Planning means that the enemy of the good is the perfect.

Planning means paying attention to our desire to be transformed.

What are the relationships you pay attention to when you plan the liturgy?

CHAPTER 4

Welcome, Experience, and Liturgy

God Is Speaking

Nobody sneaks into St. Gregory's. The front doors of the church lead into the open space of the rotunda, where the altar stands at the very center. Some people stop just inside the front doors, where an icon of Christ is there to welcome them. Others make a hard left at the entrance and head to the welcome table. We put the table to the left because people who read Western text usually scan a room from left to right, just as you're reading this page from left to right. People step inside and, if we're on our game, a St. Gregory's member will walk up and greet the visitor, offer them a nametag, give them a music book, and talk to them. That's how we begin the work of welcoming people, but it is hardly the end of the work.

Welcoming people is an easy thing if it's just about physical access to our buildings or offering people a nametag or giving them a music book and a kind word. Welcoming people is much more challenging when we admit that it is first about making room in our lives for strangers. Welcome is more challenging when we have to change the ways we are in relationship with each other—even the ways we are in relationship with God—because strangers come into our liturgies. People who have never worshiped with us carry with them both the promise of new friendship and being unknown others.

The promise is exhilarating; everyone looks forward to new friendship. Otherness is both exciting and a little scary; making room for otherness requires work. Perhaps, more than anything, welcoming otherness requires our emotional labor, which tells me that welcoming others is a spiritual practice. Before we can welcome strangers with the love of Christ, we have to prepare ourselves to be opened by them—and the Holy Spirit. And we have to be willing to hack the prayer book to make space to welcome the experiences of strangers into our worship.

This flies in the face of so much of what churches have learned over the years. We have centuries of practice about how to fix people before welcoming them, ignoring people to maintain anonymity, baptizing them before giving them communion, and erecting safe boundaries. Borders and boundaries were always being crossed by Jesus in his earthly ministry, and the same energy ought to fill the ministry of his Living Body, the church. But we often draw back from crossing boundaries.

Millenia of formation in social practice have taught humankind that the unknown other is to be feared more than welcomed. Sometimes we draw a circle around the community, repeating the lesson we learned in the beginning of human culture that the excluding circle kept insiders safe and defined what it meant to be human. As the anthropologist Claude Lévi-Strauss writes, "Humanity is confined to the borders of the tribe, the linguistic group, or even, in some instances, to the village."[1] It seems that our natural instinct is to mark a line that divides "us" from "them."

None of this is an excuse for exclusion; it's just the case that our brains are wired to suspect those we do not know. In his work *Unclean: Meditations on Purity, Hospitality, and Mortality*, Richard Beck claims, "Our affections follow our ontology. Kindness flows toward my kin, my kind. Beyond those borders are strangers and monsters. And our feelings toward these 'outsiders' range from blank indifference, to disgust, to contempt, to hatred."[2] We might choose to welcome the stranger, but both our culture and psychology consistently argue against it. The only ones whom we can safely claim as our own are people whom we know as "kin

---

1. Claude Lévi-Strauss, *Race and History* (Paris: UNESCO, 1952), 12.

2. Richard Beck, *Unclean: Meditations on Purity, Hospitality, and Mortality* (Cambridge, MA: Lutterworth Press, 2012), 140.

and kind" or who are so like us already we believe can be changed from them into "us." Too often we follow this norm, extending hospitality to people like us and suspecting everyone else of ill intent. We hardly ever think consciously this way. More often we hide our fear of others by making the church in the image of a family or by focusing only on shared interests. I can still remember the single time I heard someone at St. Gregory's say of a newcomer, "She's going to fit in just fine here—she likes the same things we all like."

Our practice is to refer to St. Gregory's as a community instead of a family. For many, family equals exclusion. Even those of us who have happy experiences of family must remember that the chief definition of family is a gathering of people we have little agency in joining. Families require closed boundaries, which maintain a warm, familiar environment. It is hard for families to accept new members as they are, without recreating them as "us." A community, though, is a mixture of unknown others and well-loved kindred. Communities are the place where strangers and kindred bump into each other and remake each other. A community could be defined as a place that you go to meet strangers.

All of which is to say that there are very good reasons that congregations have trouble welcoming strangers and their experiences. And there are critical reasons that the Episcopal Church must extend its welcome not only at the front door, but in the liturgy. According to Kristin Stache of Wartburg Theological Seminary, if we do not welcome more people into our lives, if our current decline continues, then the denomination will have no Sunday attendees in thirty years.[3] I recognize that scary statistics are never much of a motivation for welcoming strangers. God's call provides all the motivation we need, and welcoming strangers into our worship is God's call to practice hospitality not just with our kin and kind, but with everyone who comes through our doors. The living Body of Christ is not about our

---

3. "Executive Council approves readmission of Cuba, selects Louisville for 2024 General Convention," Episcopal News Service, *https://www.episcopalnewsservice.org*, accessed February 17, 2020.

preferences, but about God's love; it is God's call that constitutes the Body of Christ.

This will always challenge congregations, because as Beck plainly states, our feelings toward strangers range from blank indifference to disgust, to contempt, to hatred. God's call to welcome strangers serves to deconstruct the very natural impulses that want us to draw a closed circle. And, if our welcome is real, it means welcoming the gifts and abilities that strangers bring to us, including their experiences of liturgy.

Welcoming experience from strangers is a daily challenge that we are called to engage; it is a spiritual discipline. This discipline changes us. As Beck describes it, we become "curved outward in a catholic, universal embrace of the other."[4] The space where we respect the dignity of every human being is only occupied at great personal cost and spiritual labor. When we welcome strangers and their experiences into our congregations, it is hardly ever a cozy get together with like-minded friends; it is always the radical work given to us in the gospel and enacted in our lives.

I love this quote from Christine Pohl: "Hospitality is resistance."[5] As we welcome the experiences of strangers, we show the full extent of this resistance in our liturgy. The table fellowship of Jesus shows us that by embracing "the least," and acknowledging that as we share the same value, we are living as Christ's Body in the world. This stands in contrast to certain values of the broader community that wants to know the stranger before they can become a part of the group—or prepare them by conforming them to the experiences of insiders before we listen to the experiences they bring to us.

We have to decide how committed we are in our welcome. We have to recognize the cost that comes with our welcome. And when we mess this up beyond recognition, we have to begin anew the spiritual practice of welcoming experience. This is a lesson I have to learn over and over again.

---

4. Beck, 140.

5. Christine D. Pohl, *Making Room: Recovering Hospitality as a Christian Tradition* (Grand Rapids, MI: Eerdmans, 1999), 61.

Sermon Sharing

The practice of sermon sharing, first the preacher having their word and then the congregation having theirs, goes back to the founding of St. Gregory's. It is a part of our liturgy that fully resonates with adult models of learning practiced across the church. We don't think of people as "empty vessels" that need to be filled with data; we believe that everyone who comes to the liturgy has an experience that they can share for the sake of our mutual enrichment. Formation in the liturgy uses, as Jack Mezirow writes, "a meaning that we have already made to guide the way we think, act, or feel about what we are currently experiencing."[6] But formation in the liturgy also includes the hope of new insight. Mezirow continues, "In transformative learning, we reinterpret an old experience from a new set of expectations, thus giving a new meaning and perspective to the old experience."[7]

Formation in the liturgy, specifically in the sermon, is best served when there is a dialogic method. The preacher shares their understanding of the scriptures and their lived experience, providing a new way into the text of scripture and the text of people's experience for the listening congregation. At its best, the sermon pushes against what people have in mind when they take their seats in the pews. Then listeners are encouraged to reflect on their own lived experiences, and offer them as another text from which new meaning can be drawn. This dialogic method breaks the paradigm of the sermon as a one-way address of the preacher to each individual listener. When the liturgy gives an opportunity for people to publicly, audibly, share their stories, the rest of the congregation joins in the process of opening God's Word for the sake of transformation. One person's story prompts another's, and the whole community hears the Word of God in a fresh way.

Over the years, we have found that sermon sharing only works in this way when people share experiences instead of opinions

---

6. Jack Mezirow, *Transformative Dimensions of Adult Learning* (San Francisco: Jossey-Bass, 1991), Kindle Edition, Loc. 204–05.

7. Ibid., Loc. 213–14.

or positions. After the sermon, the preacher invites sermon sharing, using an intentional line that says: "We complete the sermon together by sharing our experiences, so if in the words spoken today you have heard something of your own story, I invite you to stand and speak. Listen to each other, and listen in the silence, because God is speaking in both." From a Mezirowian perspective, sharing opinions reflects the first movement in learning, sharing insights that we have already made. From the same learning theory, sharing stories gives the congregation an opportunity to talk about what surprises, what challenges, what sparks imagination, what opens a new understanding of the world and God's place in the world. When people share their experiences, it invariably opens space for others to do the same. It is this spark of insight, darting through the congregation, that provides new insights that the preacher didn't know when they began. The newness of sermon sharing is the reason that we like to say that, "We complete the sermon together."

At our weekly staff meetings, we always begin by talking about what happened in the prior Sunday's liturgy. We ask about what our experience was like. We talk about visitors whom we welcomed into the liturgy. We talk about logistics, liturgical supplies, hymns we liked, and all the stuff that is adjacent to the heart of the liturgy. But, more than anything else, we talk about sermon sharing. It's not uncommon for Sanford, our music director, to say, "That was a great sermon—there was such great sermon sharing."

I have witnessed sermon sharing that changed my understanding of the gospel and undermined my sense of security in an interpretation of the text. After a particularly convicting sermon about justice, I witnessed a woman kneel in the middle of the platform in front of the preacher and begin by saying to the preacher, "You bitch," and confess the power of the prophetic word to unmake her sense of privilege. I have witnessed children share about things that happen at school, and strangers talk about the power of welcome they have had that morning. I have witnessed alcoholics talk about their sobriety and mourners share their pain through tears. Sermon sharing has the power to crack open our hearts, so that we can be reformed by God's grace.

And sermon sharing is the most stressful moment of my week. After I have preached the "perfect" sermon, I open a time for people to speak about my words and make their own meaning. I worry endlessly that the first sharing will bring an opinion that will shift everyone from their hearts to their heads. I dread hearing, "I was listening to NPR," or "There was a great article in the newspaper." I pretend not to see those who raise their hands almost every week, eager to fill the silence with sharing. And I wonder when nobody says a word, "Was it such a terrible sermon that nobody has anything to say?"

Sometimes my thoughts go to the very first time I ever preached. I was fourteen years old. In my cradle denomination, the Church of Christ, people expected young men to be able to preach. The location was a nursing home, the occasion was Father's Day, and the text was the Parable of the Prodigal Son. I do not remember anything that I said in that sermon, but I remember what happened at the end: the adult who accompanied me took a moment to explain my sermon to the assembly. It was humiliating, embarrassing, and genuinely informative. Initially, the experience taught me that preaching was supposed to be a certain thing with a certain shape. It took a long time before I could leave this humiliation behind me and understand that a theology of proclamation must include more than one voice.

Any theology of proclamation worth its salt is grounded and rooted in love. The preacher must nurture a genuine concern for the transformation of every person in both the sermon and the sharing. More than anything, the preacher needs to practice the kind of engagement that draws everyone into the event of speaking gospel. The preacher and congregants are in a kind of dance, each paying attention to the others so that the steps are graceful and lead, in every moment, to see more of God. It is in the harmony of this motion that both the preacher and the assembly are formed. The stories we share in the sermon are not just personal anecdotes; they are containers of God's Word. Despite our hesitance and resistance, God wants to be known in what the preacher says and in the response of the assembly. Our imperfections do not obscure the gospel in preaching; the gospel shines through our imperfections.

The sermon is about listening to the whole community, not just what the preacher has to bring. It is not about a carefully wrapped package that leads to a proper moral ending; it is often really shabby. We listen openly for God's word in the Bible. We use the tools of critical scholarship to increase our listening. We listen for God in Christian teaching and experience, and in the wisdom of other faiths. But we don't listen to hear easy answers; we listen in the midst of the struggle that the whole assembly takes on. The art of disruption means that we consciously seek a conversation among God, the preacher, and the congregation, not establish an ideological relationship that provides quick answers to impossibly hard questions. We choose to disrupt the long-standing pattern of proclamation because God is still speaking in each of our stories, and we want to hear more of what God has to say. Sermon sharing is a beautiful moment in the liturgy—except when it's not.

From the presider's chair—the place where I sit to preach as well as preside—I can see everyone who comes in after the service begins. I saw Natalia as soon as she walked into the building, about fifteen minutes after we had begun the service. She made her way to a chair on the left side of the seating area. The first time I noticed her had been a week earlier: she seemed like a run-of-the mill visitor, somewhat hesitant but still interested.

As a community, we try our best to act like Jesus and welcome everyone without exception. But, as the rector, I can always feel myself evaluating people who come for the first time. I tell myself that this is a part of guarding the flock, containing a safe space for everyone. When I see unfamiliar people, my mind is full of questions. Are they interested in joining or just passing through? Do they have a sense of humor or not? Can they talk to other people or do they need a conversation partner assigned to them? Although I'm not proud of the way I size up our visitors, it is something I have trouble letting go of. I sometimes think of Pittman McGehee, the first priest I worked for, who would joke with me when I went to his office, "What are you here for, handouts or hang-ups?" I don't like that I evaluate people this way, but the truth is I do. It seemed like Natalia was there for something, but it was hard to tell if it was handouts or hang-ups. The word that came to me in my first experience of her was "inscrutable." Was she a person I *wanted* to welcome, or one I *had* to welcome?

On her second visit, the Sunday she walked into the service late, Natalia took part in sermon sharing. I felt a sense of dread as soon as she raised her hand to speak. I tried to balance both dread and wonder. Would she be able to join in our dance or not? The steps were not full of grace. She began by referring to a point that I had made in the sermon, then continued to offer a point-by-point critique of what I had said, and what others who had shared already said, including suggestions to a woman who had shared vulnerable information about herself.

She had that annoying habit of taking a breath in the middle of her sentences, so it was difficult for me to interrupt her with our regular signal for the end of anyone's sermon sharing, "Thank you." She went on and on, until I could finally find a pause and say, "Thank you so much for sharing today. Thank you everyone. Let's move on with our service." I was living in the liturgical moment I least liked: exercising my pastoral responsibility as the presider in shutting down the conversation. The liturgy moved along, the congregation singing an Alleluia refrain to verses from the psalms while I and the other liturgical leaders carried the gospel book through the congregation for them to greet with a touch or kiss. I came to Natalia who gave me a dead-eyed, ironic smile.

During coffee hour, I approached Natalia, who was standing by herself in the corner. "I have to apologize," I began, "I didn't explain clearly to you that sermon sharing is about experiences and not asking questions or offering critique." She nodded, "Yes. I see. Thank you." A few weeks later, the same thing happened. Natalia raised her hand to share and the preacher, not me that Sunday, invited her to speak. She shared impossibly complex thoughts and accusations against unseen tormentors.

Natalia would be absent from the liturgy for weeks or months at a stretch and then reappear, always raising her hand to participate in sermon sharing. And I would practice ignoring her request to speak. I would think of the first time I was invited to preach at St. Gregory's, a few years before the founders, Rick and Donald, hired me to work there. I was justifiably nervous about leading sermon sharing. The first few people who shared offered beautiful experiences that had been sparked by the sermon. Then a man stood up and began to critique the Dancing Saints Icon in the rotunda, "I see saints like Malcolm X but where is Saint Richard Nixon?" Sitting next to me I could hear Rick whisper, barely under his breath, "Just say thank you. Just say thank you," which I eventually managed.

The risk in sermon sharing is all about the risks we face in welcoming strangers into our congregations: we can never be sure that the gifts they bring are the gifts we want to receive. But if my Sunday mantra "God wants to be known" is true, even these disruptions and strange gifts are at work revealing God's presence. Even when sermon sharing veers to opinion and not experience, even when it is filled with paranoia, or political diatribe, or "I was listening to NPR," God wants to be known. In the liturgy we exist in a time and space that is held in God's hand, and that doesn't mean that the service will be easy or relaxing. Welcoming people's experience won't make worship easy, but it will make it real. The whole congregation is at work in the liturgy, being formed in God's love, even when things go off the rails.

Liturgy, Authority, and Giving Work Away

Our welcome of people is always about welcoming them as they are, with the experiences that they bring. When my hang-ups about "safe space" and "guarding the flock" get in the way of this, our community's core value of welcoming people's experience has the power to change me. This value is manifest in many different ways: asking people to tell their stories in the course of the liturgy, giving work away to people who may or may not know how to

do the work the way we usually do it, and gathering newcomers at the end of the service to share fifteen minutes of reflection
about the service asking the question, "What did you see?" I continually remind myself that my problems welcoming strangers are
problems that I bring to the community, not a problem that the
community insists upon. When my heart is centered on Jesus's
welcome of everyone to come and be a part of our shared life, I
can trust the love and wisdom of the community to welcome even
difficult people like Natalia.

Leadership in the liturgy is a very specific kind of thing.
Because of the agreement about church order that Anglicans and
Episcopalians have hammered out since at least the sixteenth
century, we like to keep people's roles and responsibilities closely
contained. Episcopalians, along with many other mainline denominations, define clear boundaries between laypeople and ordained
people, between presbyters and deacons and bishops, and between
adults and children. Many of these boundaries are based in apostolic teaching; some are just things that we've done so long we
believe that they are apostolic teaching.

In too many places in the liturgy, the leader is tempted to
claim authority on the basis of little more than guarding turf.
And sometimes, when this authority is challenged, the justification given by the leader is just plain silly. Instead of referenc-
ing theories of authority and leadership in the liturgy that are
at best tenuous, what would happen if we looked at the source
of authority from the perspective of the gospel? What we find
there is that authority comes not from claiming some dubious
historical precedent, but from the desire to serve. Jesus claims his
greatest authority, and then commands his followers to imitate
him as he strips down and washes his disciples' feet. This isn't a
"doormat" spirituality, but is a response made on the basis of love.
The desire of God, manifest in Jesus Christ, is that love be freely
exchanged between all people. This love is known by us not only
in affection, but also in mutual service. Making real gestures of
service is the surest way to claim authority in the church. Every
other claim is egoism.

The art of disruption means looking at leadership through the lens of the gospel. The kind of self-giving that is captured in Jesus's service to his disciples is the surest marker that leadership is authentic in the liturgy. This includes sharing authority in the liturgy. In addition to obedience to the gospel charge of service, sharing authority helps the church function robustly. When leaders share authority, particularly when we define authority as the ability to do work, the resiliency of the community increases. More people gain the kinds of skills that make them strong to do the works of Jesus both in the liturgy and in the world. This is why my core value of leadership is giving work away; I want others to have a sense of their own authority. Over the years, I have practiced this at St. Gregory's and have taught it to my students. In all of it I have learned again and again the truth that leaders and followers share a universal rule: good followers make good leaders, and bad followers make bad leaders.

Giving work away is a distinctly Anglican practice. Our tradition has always sought ways to empower the whole people of God to share ministry. When the ordained hoard leadership, the church is diminished, and we start looking less and less like who we claim to be. Real authority is found when a group agrees to accomplish a common goal, which means we all have to understand what our goals are. Good leaders are those who make themselves answerable to the rest of the group and others to follow as they will. Giving away work changes you; it has the power to transform your life. And it must be repeated that transformation isn't automatic; we must consciously embrace a path of transformation. We have to strive toward change.

The Sunday liturgy at St. Gregory's is visually stunning. We put vestments on as many participants as we can: chasubles on everyone, stoles on the ordained. In so doing, we indicate that authority and leadership is spread around as much as possible. We do this because we want to show that authority is spread throughout the congregation. If there is a job that one of us can give away, we strive to share it. We lead worship with an eye on each other, watching to see when the other person may need a bit of help. We strive to serve each other, in order to make the whole service run smoothly, so that everyone can have a whole and holy experience of prayer. Which works beautifully, even when presiders lose their nerve.

For many years, St. Gregory's held a monthly Supper Service. Even more than in the morning services, I would share leadership in this liturgy with children and youth. The service relied on everyone showing up, claiming their authority to lead, and sharing the work of making the liturgy happen. One Sunday afternoon I arrived to get ready for the service, expecting that there would be enough people to claim the work needed to accomplish the liturgy. I waited for about a quarter of an hour, and nobody came. I waited another ten minutes, and a mother and two sisters arrived. These two were relatively new to our community and had never taken leadership roles before. Because we had a practice of enacting the gospel at this service, I began to panic a little. I wondered, "How can we do the liturgy the way we had planned it with only two kids?" Ten more minutes passed—just five minutes before we were to begin. I was tempted to take control of the whole service, to change our plans so that everything would fit my idea of success. I could feel the temptation taking over my imagination. And, as always seems to happen, enough people showed up to share leadership generously. The service was beautiful.

Giving work away to people that may or may not know how to do the work the way I think it should be done makes me nervous. It feeds into one of my worst traits: wanting things to be perfect. So, on that Sunday afternoon, I started focusing on what might go wrong, instead of paying attention to everything that was going well. And as I did I began to feel more and more isolated and less joyful. I really had to stop myself, make a conscious choice not to misuse my authority, because every time I felt like things weren't going to work out, they did. The whole team of leaders did the work that we all need done to make the service work. All I had to do was pay attention to the wholeness of the community, not just to my own ego's desire to be seen as perfect.

Giving our work away means we lose some control of our lives. Giving work away means that we have to pay attention to the hope that comes when we live in relationship to each other, not the dread that comes when I feel out of control. Giving work away flies in the face of the strongest force that energizes the spirit of the age: individualism. Finding our unity by giving work away undermines our autonomy; it takes a kind of freedom away from us—the freedom to do as we please, irrespective of what others want.

I witness this attitude in the ways that people talk about liturgy on social media; oftentimes it pits one style against another and always with a side of judgment. At our worst, we tend to make other liturgical practices indicators of spiritual maturity or weakness; we categorize people on the basis of their relationship to preaching tabs or dalmatics. All of the talk of "the other" reinforces the most powerful prejudice that tempts us: that our practices and opinions matter more than any others. It seems that the only thing that matters in our liturgical discourse today is how firmly we can identify what is right and what is wrong. The spirit of the age wants to build walls between our congregations and around our hearts. The spirit of the age wants us to be strong individuals in a way that denies the gift of generosity and the power of shared leadership. The spirit of the age glories in the shameful exclusion of what it considers alien.

But beneath the surface of our individuality there is a spiritual web that connects us in unseen ways. Who you are, and who I am, are both caught up in this web. We are more *inter*dividuals than individuals. We are all related in a new humanity that comes as a gift from God: we are the Body of Christ. We can learn how to live as *inter*dividuals by paying attention to the way that Jesus Christ imagines himself in relation to God, all of which comes down to service:

> Let the same mind be in you that was in Christ Jesus, who, though he was in the form of God, did not regard equality with God as something to be exploited, but emptied himself, taking the form of a slave, being born in human likeness. And being found in human form, he humbled himself and became obedient to the point of death—even death on a cross. (Philippians 2:5–11)

When we imitate Christ's way of service, we discover that the way to live is walking side-by-side with others. The Spirit of Christ will always show us that the fullness of life is in serving and being served. In our fragile humanity, we screw it up; in our new humanity we circle back and practice service once again. What really matters is making a commitment to seeing ourselves in the other person, digging deep so that we can find the place where we can truly empathize with another person's experience.

This is different from helping someone or fixing someone. Too often, we define "helping another person" based in the assumption that the other person is weak. Most of the time, we define "fixing the problem" as fixing someone we think is broken. When you give work away, it means that you see the other person as whole and holy, full of competence, brave in exercising authority. Giving work away amplifies the connection between us: all suffering is like my suffering and all joy is like my joy. As I share authority in the liturgy, giving work away that the other can do, and letting my service be just one part of the liturgy, the whole community is transformed.

Evaluating Liturgy with Shared Experience

The moment has come; the deacon or other leader has just called out, "Let us bless the Lord," to which the people respond, "Thanks be to God." People gather their belongings and head to coffee hour, or to the exits. Another Sunday liturgy has been accomplished. Now what? How do you know if the liturgy you're leading has accomplished what you believe it needs to accomplish? After the Word has been proclaimed and the sacraments have been administered, after the people have sung their praises to God and opened their hearts in prayer, there is one more piece of work that must be done: evaluating the liturgy. This too is a piece of our work that needs to be disrupted.

Offering an informed critique of the liturgy is essential, and it needs to be informed by scholarship. But hacking the prayer book means that the way we evaluate the liturgy has to include more than just scholarship. A full evaluation of the liturgy asks if the Sunday service has worked to transform the lives of those who faithfully gather. Disrupting liturgical evaluation means listening to the wisdom of worshippers. Congregations are usually not aware of the process of evaluating the liturgy; it is something that generally takes place backstage: in staff meetings or amongst worship committees. But listening to the experiences of the members of the assembly is crucial. The question to ask to fully appreciate the liturgy is the one that fully engages people's experience: "What did you see?" This question belongs to everyone in the liturgy.

People often ask me if St. Gregory's has a worship committee. Our practice of welcoming people's experience informs my response: "The whole congregation is the worship committee." We strive to listen to the experience of everyone who comes to the liturgy. We capture this listening in sermon sharing, where individuals work with the preacher to complete the sermon. Listening also takes place among the staff, who spend a good twenty or thirty minutes at regular meetings talking about the previous Sunday's liturgies. But we also want to listen to the experience of first-time visitors and evaluate our work based on what they see, hear, touch, taste, and smell in the liturgy.

We take a more concentrated approach to listening after the service in a conversation we call "Fifteen Good Minutes." For many years we have made announcements near the end of the liturgy: after we sing our blessings to those with birthdays and anniversaries, and before we sing and dance our final hymn. We encourage people to sign our guest book and talk about events that are happening after the liturgy. We mention at least one way to connect to the community in the coming week and invite anyone who wants to join in Fifteen Good Minutes to gather in a circle of chairs on the side of the church. We particularly encourage visitors to come. About ten minutes into coffee hour, someone rings the tower bell, and people gather to debrief the liturgy.

We always begin by asking the question, "What did you see?" In our long experience as a congregation, we have learned that it is always better to ask questions about people's sensory experience of the service as opposed to people's opinions about it. The impression that the liturgy makes on a person is enough to reveal new insight about God and the world.

This phenomenon is primary liturgical theology. Gordon Lathrop writes, "Primary liturgical theology is the communal meaning of the liturgy exercised by the gathering itself. The assembly uses combinations of words and signs to speak of God."[8] Everyone who attends the liturgy, old-timers and newcomers, theological sophisticates and theological beginners, children and adults, all possess theological imaginations and are competent to do primary liturgical theology. We find that welcoming people into the theological task through their senses is the first step in the transformative process in their lives.

Evaluating the liturgy is a theological task, a way of reflecting on the experience of God and the world that we encounter in worship. The theological reflection we make out of the liturgy is always about the meaning of people's experience in worship. Theological reflection on the liturgy is not merely a quick review of the Sunday service. If we want to evaluate what we are doing in the liturgy, we must strive to understand what is happening in the lives of those who come to worship. Evaluation of the liturgy must be more than, "We made it through, and nobody died." Evaluating the liturgy takes us into the deep waters where we have to critique the liturgical traditions we cling to so dearly and ask if they are practices in which people experience transformation or that they just endure.

The liturgy is theological because it works in the lives of worshipers to make communal meaning out of what we do in worship. Making meaning is both primary theology, where the event of the liturgy reveals God, and secondary theology, where reflecting on the worship experience enables us to have a more profound understanding of the liturgy. We come to church and catch a sense of God's presence in the beauty, words, and actions of the liturgy;

---

8. Gordon Lathrop, *Holy Things: A Liturgical Theology* (Minneapolis: Fortress, 1999), 5.

all of these have the power to change us in the moment. We also take this beauty, these words and actions, with us into the world, and continue to chew on them until new meanings emerge. These insights form in us an ability to understand both the world and God more fully. This is the work that transforms us.

The liturgy itself is insufficient to reveal God because only God can reveal God. But it is in the liturgy that God desires to be revealed. Evaluating the liturgy must begin with love. The love of God poured out in Jesus Christ, made available by the power of the Holy Spirit, is the meeting place where our theological reflection on the liturgy is most fruitful. Again, this process is intimately related to sharing and welcoming each other's lived experiences. Because we realize love as an experience instead of an idea, we evaluate the liturgy in the context of people's lives in worship. The stakes in this kind of reflection are high; the pressing question is not simply, "Did we do everything the right way?" The pressing issue is about our encounter with the God of love. The very best question to ask is, "Where did you experience God in worship?" As Michael B. Aune writes of Orthodox liturgical theology, "The liturgy is a *present encounter* with God. Salvation is now. It is this *present-ness* and *now-ness* that mark the realism of the liturgy of Byzantine Orthodox Christians—that it is an event of an active, faith encounter *now* with the *present* saving activity of Christ."[9] Our evaluation of the liturgy must engage the assembly in the moment of worship and so transform them into a new people before God.

Asking people about their experiences of what has just happened in the liturgy, grounded in their senses, can give the most honest answer to the question of what people believe matters in worship. When we ask people, "What did you see?" they might say, "It smells funny in church," or "I felt another person's hand on my shoulder," or "The sound of the music touched me deeply." It is simpler for people to turn to an opinion if we ask the question,

---

9. Michael B. Aune, "The Current State of Liturgical Theology: A Plurality of Particularities," *St. Vladimir's Theological Quarterly* 53 (2009): 219.

"What did you think?" Then we might hear words that stop the conversation: "I didn't like it," "I disagreed with the sermon," or "I thought it was pretty cool."

It is difficult, if not impossible, to faithfully evaluate the liturgy based on opinion. Our opinions operate in one of two ways: opinions either tend to disconnect people from each other, or they shrink our sense of meaning by limiting our engagement to people who are just like us. But sharing opinions, as opposed to experiences, maintains an impression of safety. In other words, opinions isolate us, which makes our lives smaller. The liturgy is given to us in order to strengthen connection, connection in both human and divine terms. Too often, there is a profound disconnection between people's experience of the liturgy and their experience of God. But the liturgy promises us more.

We are creatures of God designed to live in mutual relationships that connect us to one another and to the God who creates us. We are designed to live together in relationships of profound connection, and any force that threatens this fundamental, essential part of our being unmakes us. We are living in an era of profound disconnection in the world. Violence and rejection emerge easily, and vulnerability is rejected. It becomes easy to scapegoat the other if we do not see their neediness as a part of our own experience. And I get it: the cost of connection is the messiness of living with people who are different from me, with whom I want to have no connection. It is so much easier to simply identify them as other, and move on to their expulsion, either literally or in my imagination.

Over the years, St. Gregory's has put a priority on welcoming experience. We strive to listen to how God is speaking to us in the words that are spoken by those who come to worship with us. We have taken the experiences that people share and made changes to the liturgy. We evaluate the liturgy on the basis of people's experiences of worship to make abundantly clear that the relationship between what we do in worship and the experience of God alive in the world has the power to transform us. And more than anything, we want to be made new.

A Symbolic Universe for Insiders and Outsiders

My dream job would be the liturgical consultant for filmmakers. The media doesn't depict liturgy very well; when there's some worship service in a movie, they tend to get the details wrong, like putting a red stole on the priest performing a wedding. Or when actors wear their chasubles backward. And I find it distracting when there are novelty candles on the altar instead of the proper kind and number. All this makes me crazy because I have internalized a symbolic universe of meaning that moviemakers don't care about. Most movies care about a different reality than the one I think should matter.

The term "symbolic universe" is a way of describing the unseen structures and traditions that provide human beings with meaning and symbolically order our institutions.[10] A symbolic universe links different areas of meaning in people's lives; it creates order in a world that is chaotic and gives people tools with which to make meaning. More than that, it gives an explanation and justification to the relational world within which people live, including the liturgy.

For Christians, the symbolic universe is grounded in the story of salvation. This story explains reality and gives integrity to the liturgy. The story of salvation shapes the words and actions of worship and weaves them together so that they transform our lives. The story of salvation puts everything in its right place. The seasons and symbols we encounter in liturgy unify our worship, teach us how to understand life, and tell us how to serve God in the world. And when we stray from this reality, the story of salvation has the power to bring us back to our right minds.

As with badly staged worship in movies, we cannot take for granted that the larger cultures within which we live understand any of this. The words, actions, seasons, and symbols that shape reality in the liturgy may be completely opaque to those outside our life in worship. We do not live in a world that has a shared

---

10. Peter L. Berger and Thomas Luckmann, *The Social Construction of Reality: A Treatise in the Sociology of Knowledge* (New York: Anchor Books, 1966/1990), 106.

symbolic universe, which we have to remember when we welcome people into the liturgy. We cannot assume that people know what we mean by words like "eucharist" or "Paschal Mystery" or "prayers." These are realities that people have to practice for them to have meaning. People who don't come to the liturgy may hear about liturgy, and without experiencing it, find it meaningless and alienating. I can tell people the meaning of the eucharist, but without receiving the bread and wine that are Christ's body and blood, it may sound like something akin to cannibalism.

The art of disruption tells me that welcoming the unprepared to fully participate in the liturgy is critical in sharing the story of salvation. Excluding the unprepared from full participation in the liturgy is a crisis. And because crisis is the time in which God is always active, this means that we are being invited by the Holy Spirit to tear up our plans and start over. We have to find new ways of welcoming the unprepared to share in our words, actions, seasons, and symbols, and of opening up the rest of the treasury that fills the liturgy.

The church used to take for granted that the same symbols formed everyone. The church tells stories rooted in a matrix of meanings that we assume everyone understands. In the past, we used these stories to form and regulate time and space. For example, when you heard bells tolling, sounding a bell slowly with a significant pause between strikes, you knew someone had died. Early in my ordained ministry, working at Christ Church Cathedral in Houston, I learned about the "funeral toll" from Ardell Ray, the cathedral sexton. Whenever we had a funeral, he would stand in the bell porch of the cathedral as pallbearers brought the casket into the building, with a serious expression on his face, silently counting between each tug of the bell-rope. He took his work seriously, because the burial of the dead is more than a moment of personal sadness; it recalls the whole community to both the pain of death and the power of the resurrection. Ardell would pull the bell-rope and count, "one, two, three" and then slowly pull it again. The deep reverberation of sound bounced off neighboring skyscrapers. That sound, as deep as our grief and persistent as our hope, meant that it was time to pay attention; it was a permission to pause and pay respect.

Today, in many places, people don't know what it means if you hear bells tolling. There is rarely a public summons to grieve. Church bells may sound impressive, but for many people they lack meaning. I don't believe that we have become impervious to grief, but we lack a shared language to talk about grief. The church's ritual actions have the power to connect people whose hearts are cracked open by grief. When we cease to share these powerful symbols, we leave people with only their grief and no word of hope. People will not understand our symbols unless we more clearly communicate their meaning, sharing both the reality of grief and the hope of resurrection. If we want to welcome those outside our doors to come and see what we believe, we must learn to communicate the meaning of our rituals and symbols.

Creating liturgy in the time of COVID-19 has challenged so much of what we take for granted about worship, ritual actions, and our symbolic universe. So many people have been sickened by the novel coronavirus, and too many have died. Instead of anointing the sick for healing, we have had to talk to them on mobile phones and in Zoom rooms. Instead of gathering to cense the caskets of the dead and shower them with baptismal water, we draw back from complex ritual for the sake of public health. Instead of bearing witness at the cremation of our beloved dead, we wait anxiously for their remains to arrive by the U.S. Postal Service. The story of salvation continues to offer comfort in the face of sickness and death, but we have learned to tell the story in ways that avoid contact with the dead and grieving. The structures and traditions that have formed our liturgical imaginations continue to form us, but how we express these has changed.

The first time that I presided at a burial in the pandemic, it was for a woman who had died from COVID-19. She and her mother had been members of St. Gregory's years before, and she had moved away long before I came to serve the congregation. But when she died, her mother asked for her ashes to be interred in our columbarium. The county health department had yet to

lift the quarantine on worship gathering inside religious buildings, so we met outdoors. The county had also limited the number of people who could assemble for burial, so we were a small
group of mourners.

There were only five people present for the service, and no
family members; we livestreamed the service via Zoom tele-
conferencing. I set up a computer monitor outside the building,
by the large, dark green rock that is our baptismal font. One by
one, observing physical distancing, members of the small assembly would stand in front of the monitor, before the dead woman's scattered family. As we always had done before at burials, we
each placed flowers at the urn of ashes. I said the prayers, and
my colleague, Donald Schell, preached the homily. We carried
the ashes to the columbarium, and I committed my beloved sister,
a stranger to me, to God's care and keeping. Then we gathered
again in front of the monitor to speak to the family.

All of the symbols—placing flowers, praying together, hearing the Word read and proclaimed, interring the ashes—were
present with us and visible to those who could not be there. And
I remembered what a colleague shared with me of her experience
officiating at a burial in the pandemic. "When it was over, all I
wanted to do was to hug them," she told me, "and I couldn't." It
reminded me of what a friend had said years before, when he was
isolated because of prolonged illness, "It's like I have skin hunger."
The inability to be present with, let alone embrace the dead woman's grieving family, was like a wound that couldn't heal. If I could
have reached through the screen and touched them, I would have.

The liturgy operates in a symbolic universe that continues
to offer refuge and the chance to return to God, but in the pandemic, our ritual actions challenge public safety. For the first time
in generations, so many of the ritual actions we take for granted
are not permitted by those who strive against the pandemic. Still,
the rituals surrounding death help construct reality when our
beloved friends die. Our work is to talk about these actions with
those who approach the end of life. If we do not take this pastoral,
liturgical theology seriously, death is rendered antiseptic and even

more strange. Death is more than a bad thing that happens in a random pandemic; it is birth to eternal life. The liturgy for the dead contains a genius that the death care industry cannot touch. For the love of the resurrection, we must share our symbols and rituals generously with everyone.

Trusting Our First Principles

Everything that we have faced in the time of the pandemic invites us to return to first principles. Years ago I was talking to my mother about some research I was doing in the field of liturgics. I explained some technical sense of the sociological purpose of the Sunday liturgy—I may even have used the word *ordo*—and she just looked at me the way my mother looks at me when she both loves me and doesn't understand me. When I was finished she said, "I just thought worship was about pleasing God."

The first principle of our worship is pleasing God. And when I forget this, I get wrapped up in issues that are not important, like having a perfect performance of the liturgy. I also forget that worship is given for the pleasure of those who gather. Our task is to share our liturgy as clearly and lovingly as we can so that it fosters joy, even in the face of loss and isolation. The most surprising thing to me about online liturgy in the pandemic was seeing the faces of people, physically distant from me, but also present. The pleasure of their company was transformative; it showed me the face of God.

The meaning of the liturgy is always found in the wisdom of Jesus. Throughout the gospels, Jesus offers a vision of his Abba's rule, more often called the Kingdom of Heaven. This rule is first of all about forgiveness, truth, and welcome to those easily written off as lost. This rule excludes nothing but what demeans the weak, meek, and little. This rule orients all humanity on the path that leads to knowing God as intimately as Jesus knows God. This knowledge frees us to let go of what is oppressive, egocentric, and atavistic. All of this is expressed in the loving relationship that Jesus shares with his Abba. Which tells me that the art of disrupting the liturgy must be done in relationships of love. The art of disruption means taking the liturgy and using images, language, movement, space, and time that amplify grace, mercy, compassion, love, and forgiveness. If these are not the things that shape the liturgy, we have to deconstruct it and start over again. And when we do this, we must welcome everyone to join in fully, without exception.

My friend Charles Rotramel runs an organization called Revision; they work with people that he calls "disconnected youth." These are young people who have been on a trajectory toward homelessness, addiction, crime, sex-trafficking, incarceration, joblessness, gang membership, and suicide. The people who volunteer with these disconnected youth have no agenda other than to show up in compassion, pay attention without distraction, and listen without judgment.

Revision is based in a neighborhood where many immigrants and refugees live. One of the kids in the neighborhood was born in Somalia, a part of a group of young men who were raised in refugee camps in Africa. Everyone knew that this kid was bad. He was always high, dealing drugs, engaged in sex work. The kids who were already in the program said that this guy just couldn't come to their meetings, all of which began by sitting at a table and sharing a meal. Charles told them, "We have to let him join us at dinner or he will die." Charles found the young man and asked him to join them for dinner. Charles sat him at the center seat of the long dinner table and told him, "We want you to be a part of Revision, if you want to be." The kid, who always sat looking at his feet, jerked his head up and said, "I'm a part of Revision?" Charles said, "Yes. You can eat here."

Here's what Charles didn't say: you have to stop being a bad kid; you have to stay away when you're high; you have to wait to get a background check. They didn't ask the bad kid to become the good kid before he could eat. He didn't have to do anything, but keep coming. All he had to do was eat with them. This is the way that God welcomes us to come to the liturgy, and it is in this welcome that we see the nature of God.

Sitting at the table, eating with those who are bad, who are not prepared, who have not yet changed their behavior, who may never change their behavior, this is a part of the symbolic universe of the liturgy. For the liturgy to have any meaningful future, we have to disrupt it and strive to share it with both insiders and outsiders. We must do this work in partnership with those who aren't in church, deliberately and consciously. We have to listen to the stories of everyone who comes to us, and we have to do it consistently for as long as we are gathering for worship. We have to construct reality in the Spirit of Jesus, the Spirit of grace, mercy, compassion, love, and forgiveness. We have to look for the ways that these practices are being expressed in the world outside of church, and we have to learn how to talk about these in ways that are transformative for those who are inside the church and for those who are coming closer to church. And we have to do it today.

This is what I'm learning about welcoming experience in the liturgy . . .

Welcoming strangers into the church will change the church.

The Word of God is alive in the words people share in the liturgy.

My leadership in the liturgy is only as strong as my willingness to give work away.

People become more deeply connected when they share their experiences.

We must learn to share the symbols of the liturgy with everyone.

Something is happening outside the church that we must know.

What might you do to begin welcoming people's experiences in the liturgy and sharing the symbols of the liturgy with strangers?

CHAPTER 5

Death, Resurrection, and Liturgy

The Necessity of Hope

One of the most critical tasks for the church today is to nurture hope. Congregational life is hard, and the chances are it's not going to get easier anytime soon. In many places, money is tight, membership is down, and attendance is sporadic. According to Dwight Zscheile, vice president of innovation and associate professor of congregational mission and leadership at Luther Seminary in St. Paul, Minnesota, "At this rate, there will be no one in worship by around 2050 in the entire denomination."[1] According to some estimates, the Episcopal Church faces a considerable clergy shortage; by 2023, there will be half the number of active priests needed for the almost 6,500 congregations in the denomination. And then there is the so-called "death tsunami" coming in North American culture. A decade ago, the website Ministry Matters predicted that "between 2019 and 2050, there will be more deaths and a higher death rate than at any time since the 1940s when medical advances such as antibiotics were introduced."[2] The website also reported that "the total number of deaths each year is predicted to go up every year until 2050 as Baby Boomers pass away."[3]

---

1. Egan Millard, "2019 Parochial Reports Show Continued Decline and a 'Dire' Future for the Episcopal Church," Episcopal News Service, *https://www.episcopalnewsservice.org/2020/10/16/2019-parochial-reports-show-continued-decline-and-a-dire-future-for-the-episcopal-church/*, accessed October 17, 2020.

2. Lovett H. Weems Jr., "The Coming Death Tsunami," Ministry Matters, *https://www.ministrymatters.com/all/entry/1868/the-coming-death-tsunami*, accessed February 22, 2020.

3. Ibid.

If you listen to the larger system in which we live, you will hear messages that say that you are already a little bit dead. Maybe the message is that you don't have enough money, or enough time, or enough energy, or enough love, or enough beauty. Or perhaps the culture tells you that everybody else is dying, but you have nothing to worry about because you have saved enough money, or gone to the gym religiously enough, or you're living safely enough to escape harm. The culture of "the world, the flesh, and the devil"[4] is invested in our anxiety about death, or at least in the kinds of loss that bring the fear of death to mind.

This cultural message is powerful and penetrates every institution, including the church. Declining member rolls, diminishing attendance, and shrinking donations too often steer our attention to what seems like the inevitability of the church's demise. It seems there is always a little bit of death hanging around our churches and often in our hearts. But there is a silver lining to the cloud of death: we really can't talk about the Resurrection if we don't face our fear of death. The Resurrection is the birthing place of hope.

Hope needs to be nurtured. Amid decline and death, when it seems the best we can do is just show up and make it through the myriad challenges of creating liturgy, the Resurrection may be the last thing we consider. The art of disruption wants to show that the liturgy is always about the Resurrection. Or, as we say at St. Gregory's, there are only two seasons on the church calendar: "Easter" and "Easter is coming." When we focus our attention on the promise of the Resurrection, the liturgy comes alive. This contrasts with the system within which our congregations exist, which is obsessed with death.

Here is a story that must clarify the church's relationship to death. A long time ago, three women hurried through the early darkness of a spring morning to care for the dead body of a friend. It was simply what they would have done for anyone dear to them. When they arrived, they discovered that the certainty of death had broken down; their dead friend was not in the tomb

---

4. A phrase from the Great Litany in the 1928 Book of Common Prayer.

in which they had placed him. The security that the dead stay dead was overturned; he was gone. Instead, there was a strange young man in a white robe sitting on the burial stone. He said to the frightened witnesses, "Do not be alarmed; you are looking for Jesus of Nazareth, who was crucified. He has been raised; he is not here. Look, there is the place they laid him" (Mark 16:6). Through a haze of wondering, the three women left the tomb in fear and kept quiet. It would be some time before they began to tell everyone who would listen that death had lost its power. But first, the women were afraid.

The story of the Resurrection begins with fear, just as we may fear the approach of death. The fear that came to those brave witnesses at the empty tomb was not only about their friend's death; it was about the unsettling sense that death had been undone. Maybe they, like us, were so accustomed to the presence of death that they didn't know what to do when they were freed from its power. For my part, some days it feels like I've gotten so used to being a little bit dead that I forget what Christ's Resurrection has won for us. Well, here it is: "Christ is risen from the dead, trampling down death by death, and giving life to those in the tomb."[5] This isn't just good news for those who have already met their mortal end. All of us who may feel a little bit dead have been given a new kind of life, which means that the little versions of death that get woven into our stories aren't the final word for us. There is no shame so demeaning that the power of the Resurrection hasn't made it impotent. There is no fear so great that the power of the Resurrection hasn't rendered it ridiculous. There is no sense of scarcity so pervasive that the power of the Resurrection hasn't mocked it thoroughly. Hope is born in the power of the Resurrection.

But before hope is born in us, we have to be honest about how afraid we really are. If we don't acknowledge that fear, that gut-wrenching fear that creeps up on us when we least expect it, then it is hard to understand the power of the Resurrection. Thanks be to God, there are myriad signs of the Resurrection

---

5. Book of Common Prayer, 500.

around us, signs of its power to overturn death. Just as your 3:00 a.m. fear is dispelled by the first light of day, so the fear of death is kicked to the curb by the power of the Resurrection. Just like your guilt over past failures is overcome by the unconditional love of another, so the fear of death is made unnecessary by the power of the Resurrection. Just like your fear that you might be turned away from God's presence is ridiculed by Christ's welcome to the feast, so the fear of death is obliterated by the power of the Resurrection. Despite our fear, hope is available to all who seek it out. This is the context in which we practice the art of disruption and hacking the prayer book: Easter is coming. If we want to use the liturgy to nurture hope, we must be ready to take a hard look at death.

Looking Hard and Editing Out

I have painted since I was about nine years old. Over the years I have found that I have good visual intelligence: I can discern colors well, know the fundamental canon of design, and can look at a view and form an opinion of its aesthetic value. But seeing and painting are two very different things. For a couple of years in college, I studied art before turning to religion and psychology as my major fields. My teachers tried to get all of us students to see before asking us to paint or draw. One of my teachers had us look at crumpled brown paper bags and then draw them. That assignment asked us to look intently at something so commonplace that we simply took for granted what it looked like. My teacher insisted that we look hard at the crumpled brown paper bag before we reproduce it in chalk on paper. This "looking hard at something" is one of the lessons I recall from studying art. I was taught to create an image of what I actually saw in front of me, not what I imagined was in front of me.

The other lesson from art school was not to draw or paint literally. A verbatim image isn't very interesting. You can never paint everything that a view contains, nor should you try. When I was a child, I would draw a tree to look like a green ball on a brown stick because that's what I believed trees looked like. But if you take a hard look at a tree, you see that the color is complex and the lines that make sense of the color are intricate. It isn't green; it's gray and yellow and brown, and its shape is jiggly lines and patches of lightness and darkness composed of individual leaves and limbs and bark. But if you try and capture all of that in a painting, you will just make a mess; you can't paint every individual leaf and every piece of bark, it's too much. Even if you could capture every detail perfectly, the viewer wouldn't be able to take it all in. Making liturgy, like making art, is about looking hard at life, editing out what distracts from the Resurrection, and creating something that beautifully tells the truth about God, the world, and humankind.

Sometimes I forget this. I don't always follow the practice of looking hard and editing out; the same challenges that I face in painting are the ones I have in the liturgies for the dead. Sometimes I cannot see what is in front of me and edit out the parts of the liturgy that hinder transformation. I can't always connect the purpose of the liturgy with the pastoral circumstances in front of me. I can't always leave behind my preconceived ideas of how the liturgy should go with the reality of what is right in front of me. Sometimes my preconception takes over my imagination because I am pastorally tone-deaf; sometimes it's because of my natural fear of death. As it is in painting, so it is in the art of disrupting the prayer book: to see, you have to look hard and know what to add and what to leave out.

Early in my ordained ministry, I was asked to lead a graveside burial service for a family that was only tangentially connected to the parish. The godmother of one of the grieving family members arranged for me to officiate a couple of days before the service. Although I met with the godmother, I never spoke to any of the family members. She described a family alienated by abandonment, resentment, and everything that comes with the pain of broken relationships. The funeral was on a cold, wet winter afternoon. I arrived at the cemetery before the family, got out of my car, put on my cassock and surplice and a white stole. I waited for the family to arrive, reviewing the few notes I had made for the service: "Father died, mother alive, daughter estranged. Sentences, Collect, Romans 8, Psalm 23, Prayers, Commendation, Committal, Dismissal."

After a few minutes, two black town cars and a black hearse drove up. Four people got out of the two vehicles: three from one, one from the other. There were no pallbearers, so the funeral director and his assistants had to manage the coffin. I had never seen any of the family members before; their faces were tense, their eyes staring away from each other. There was something unspoken amongst them; the pain that bound them together weighed down on us like the gray clouds above our heads. I greeted the elder of the two women who shook my hand briefly. "I'm sorry for your loss," I said. She said nothing. Everyone looked at the ground as I began the service. Before the Committal, I asked if anyone would like to speak. Silence. I gave the dismissal, and they returned to their black town cars and drove away. "What am I doing here?" I wondered.

I remember this story because it is the clearest example of abject liturgical failure in my experience. Not only did I fail to look hard at what the liturgy needed, but I also failed to edit out what wasn't needed. I told myself that I didn't have time for the pastoral work of planning the liturgy. I said to myself that the majesty of the burial office would carry everyone along and accomplish what it intended to in the mourners' lives. I believed that the improvisation of asking people to speak at the graveside would be well received. It was a ritual failure. My immaturity, as well as the pain of the family, made me more afraid of the power of death than the hope of the Resurrection. So I couldn't connect the pain of the grieving family to the promise of new life. Families are torn apart by death, and when they come to the service for their beloved, too often they only have the dimmest idea that the burial office is a service of the Resurrection. Too often it is an event that simply has to be endured.

Maybe this situation is our fault—those of us who have the responsibility to shepherd mourners. Maybe we've lost our nerve and abdicated our pastoral and liturgical roles to funeral directors and other members of the death care industry. Maybe we've just stopped believing in the power of the Resurrection. But we have to do better than simply offering mourners some version of a "celebration of life." We have to offer something more than that sad feeling that comes from listening to Leonard Cohen's "Halleluiah"—which is a great song—but it isn't about the Resurrection. We have to press into eternal hope, claim the fullness of the new life promised in baptism, and give people a place to see that death is utterly transformed by life. Granted, we want mourners to be soothed by the best ritual we can produce. But the liturgist's first job is to proclaim the Resurrection and the hope of new life that flows from it.

We must disrupt the prayer book liturgies around death and welcome the power of the Resurrection that breaks upon us like the dawn. And to see the power of the Resurrection in these moments, you have to see what death looks like and what it requires of us liturgically. We have to face our fears and confess our hopelessness. We have to trust that God shows up in our neediness and in the heartrending grief that comes with death. We have to claim the prayer book's Burial of the Dead is more beautiful, honest, and real than a secular celebration of life.

The entire life of liturgy is like the painter's life. First, you have to learn to see, looking at the world with open eyes and hearts, paying attention to your life so that you can honestly know your desire. Second, you have to let go of everything that is not needed in the moment, which is our hesitance and fear. Finally, you have to pray, knowing that God is always full of mercy. When you start to see things as they are, not as you imagine they are, then you will be open to seeing the power of the Resurrection.

First Comes the Dying

My father died at sunrise on a quiet October morning in 2018. We had prayed for his healing, but sometimes cancer does not spontaneously regress, and people die. Nevertheless, as I also know, grace happens in death. This is how my father died. The night before, my siblings and mother and I gathered around him. We told stories. We shared what he had meant to each one of us. We told him that we loved him. My mother, then each one of us, gave him our permission to let go of his life. I experienced the truth that I have known my whole life, but which is most powerfully present in moments like this: those who put their trust in God will receive the gift of peace, which is a kind of healing. Our ultimate surrender into God's presence means our complete healing and our entry into unambiguous life.

After we gave him our permission to die, we all gathered around him and prayed for him. He sat in the easy chair that still sits in my parents' den, the one I can barely bring myself to sit in today; my father's chair. We knelt around him and placed our hands on him, on his head and shoulders and legs. Although it was a role I had tried to abdicate with my father's dying, I was the priest so I spoke the words of prayer. I had wanted to be my father's son, not my family's priest. But the calling to which I gave my heart all those years ago makes it hard to say "no" to the request to pray. If I could recall the words of the prayer, I would write them here, but I cannot. All I can remember is my family surrounding my father, our hands pressed against his diminished body.

It was a scene not unlike the one that had played out a few months before my father's death. I had returned to my hometown of Houston to see him. He was too-slowly dying from pancreatic cancer. We had purchased a recliner that he could get in and out of easily, that had a motor allowing the chair to be adjusted in endless variations, including one in which he could sleep comfortably. My older brother happened to be in town when I visited, so he and I got my father from his chair in the den into his wheelchair and then into the recliner so that he could sleep. And although he had expressed hope that he could sleep comfortably in the recliner, he had trouble adjusting it in a way that would relieve his pain. "My shoulder hurts," he cried. He asked for more morphine even though my mother had just given him a third, oral dose. "I can't give you anymore," she said through frustrated, frightened tears. She called my brother and me into the bedroom to help calm my father. I knelt by the chair and used the switch to slowly raise the back of the chair into a more upright position. I encouraged my father to take some deep breaths of the oxygen through the tube to his nose. And then I did for my father what he had done for me as a child when he would put me to bed: I reached my hand behind him, put it on his hurting shoulder, and began to rub it gently.

Touch. Prayer requires touch. Healing requires touch. Dying requires touch. The most vulnerable rubrics in the Book of Common Prayer all have to do with touch: joining hands in matrimony, marking the forehead with ashes for repentance, laying hands on heads at ordination, the warm embrace or formal handshake at the Peace. We have lived and died through a pandemic that was contained by holding back our touch. Sometimes the act of touch must be restrained, but the desire—the necessity—of touch cannot be forgotten.

I learned about vulnerability in my father's dying. I had to embrace the vulnerability of comforting him with my physical contact, and he had to embrace the vulnerability of his weakened body being touched by me. We might want to ignore the pain and messy physicality of death, but to do so is to deny the reality of death. Being so close to the dying is a gift and one that I am grateful I received from my father. My whole family learned about the power of human touch in my father's dying, and in this, we all came closer to the power of the Resurrection.

The art of disruption requires our vulnerability. If we want to see transformation in people's lives, we have to make ourselves vulnerable to their pain. Vulnerability is so much more than pastoral expertise or professional experience, as valuable as those are. Vulnerability is acting in the life of another person without quite knowing what is going to happen. Vulnerability opens us to new ways of acting in others' lives; it opens us to see new signs of the Resurrection and new ways to find our common life in the New Life of Christ. The First Letter of John tells us about this vocation of vulnerability: "Little children, let us love, not in word or speech, but in truth and action" (1 John 3:18). When we are present with other people, actively sharing in their struggles, we are enacting the power of the Resurrection with them, sustained by the Spirit of Christ. That kind of presence only comes as we make ourselves vulnerable, knowing our neediness. If you have no neediness, no need of another, then the Resurrection will seem oddly unnecessary. But each one of us is needy, and each one of us has the power to care for the neediness of the other.

Prayer is not just about saying the right thing in the right way at the right time, although it can include all of that. Prayer is always about our bodies, about the way that we touch each other. The theology of the Incarnation says that God's presence with us in human flesh was not a "Plan B" that God somehow managed to pull off at the last minute. Incarnation was God's gracious will from before the beginning of creation, and because human bodies are always places of suffering and humiliation, God's plan all along was to be with us in vulnerability. If you claim nothing else about God, claim this: God knows the risk and power of vulnerability. Prayer is becoming so vulnerable to the hope of God's presence that you do things that seem impossible.

I spent the final night of my father's life in the bedroom with him and my mother. I slept little, fitfully. At some point, I opened my eyes and saw through the bedroom window that the sun had risen and that my father was completely still. I knew that my father would be awake if light was coming into the bedroom. My father would rise with the rising sun, ready to live another day. And, in his stillness, I knew that he had died. I went to his side and felt for his pulses; his hand was cool, his pulses were absent. Then I did what seemed best in that moment: I leaned over and kissed his forehead, which was cool and still. There were many other scenes that morning of vulnerability and compassionate presence, but kissing my father's forehead is the one that stays with me. The heartbreaking beauty of the Resurrection was revealed to me in that moment, and I silently repeated the Easter troparion, "Christ is risen from the dead, trampling down death by death, and to those in the tombs bestowing life."

Prayers for the dying, prayers at the graveside, and the burial office require us both to be vulnerable to the fear of death that surrounds us and parry that fear with hope in the Resurrection. God asks us to look hard at death and see that it is about much more than our fear. God asks us to come to the dying and the dead who lie before us and see them as they are, not just as we expect to see them. God's invitation is to pay attention to the way that the Resurrection always eclipses death.

Tragedy and Temptation

The approach of death is not something we only address in the lives of those we know and love. Death also comes to us in highly public ways in which the church is called to respond. It may be a mass shooting, or a case of police brutality, or the overwhelming death of the pandemic. In whatever way death approaches, the church must respond to civic tragedy with liturgies that trust in the power of the Resurrection. Welcoming people in times of crisis is nothing new for the Episcopal Church. Following the 1941 bombing of Pearl Harbor, churches across the country became locations for public mourning, even for people who did not think of themselves as particularly religious. However, that was an era in which such displays of civic piety were more culturally normative; attending religious services was expected.

In most places today, attending religious services is entirely optional, and in some areas it is counter-cultural. And yet, when events have terrified members of the American public, they have turned to houses of worship as places to seek solace and comfort. The attacks of September 11, 2001, offer evidence of this. Churches worldwide held liturgies either on the day of the attacks or shortly after. With little time to prepare a liturgy, many congregations improvised around a eucharistic service. People lined up at the doors of churches an hour before they were unlocked and filled every open spot. Responding to times of civic tragedy is a time of temptation as well. The temptation is to forsake the power of the Resurrection for the power of nationalism. The art of disruption, at these times of national catastrophe, means remembering the gospel above all else; anything less tempts us to disaster.

Ten years after the attacks, I took our dog, Frankie, to the beach for an early morning walk. It was windy. San Francisco Bay was covered in whitecaps, and the sand blew fast across the whole width of the beach. Salt was blowing in the air; when we had finished our walk and got into the car for the drive home, I could taste salt in my throat. And that's when it happened. That's when memory took over from a regular Saturday morning walk with the dog. The taste of salt in my throat took me back ten years when the taste of salt in my throat was caused by spending the day swallowing my tears. At the time, I was the rector of St. Andrew's Episcopal Church in Houston. The day before had been the opening day of our new Montessori school, a moment of high hope and great expectation. After all of the crashes and collapses and all of the death, I spent that Tuesday morning talking to parents who came to get their children. One cried in my arms, "I just want to go. I just want to go somewhere that's safe." My tears came later, leaning my head into the chest of my husband Grant, staining his blue Brooks Brothers shirt. But the hardest thing was the next Sunday, struggling between the call to nationalism and the hope of the Resurrection.

I spent hours planning the Sunday liturgy. I heard my people's anger and fear, and despair. I prepared a liturgy to strike that balance between sorrow and courage and compassion that I believed we needed. And I chose to keep any hint of nationalism out of the liturgy. I chose to strive, hoping against hope, that the poison of nationalism might be leached out of people's hearts if it was absent from the liturgy. I went so far as hiding the American flag that I had put away in the sacristy when I arrived in the parish more than a year before. But when I arrived at the church at about 6:30 on Sunday morning, Bob Johnson had found it and laid it out on a table, smoothing out the wrinkles I had unintentionally left. "I think people will feel better if we have the flag today," he said; I returned the flag to its former location in the church.

At both services that day, I preached about the need to forgive, as well as to grieve. We sang hymns that were familiar and well loved. There was a larger than usual crowd at both services.

When the final liturgy was over, I took my regular place at the front door of the church, greeting people I knew and people I'd never seen before. Most were sweet and crushed and bewildered. One, an English woman in her late eighties, said, "Thank you for playing 'O God Our Help in Ages Past.' You know we would sing that during the Blitz."

But some were angry. Angry at life, angry at me. One woman demanded, "Where was our anthem?" At first I assumed she meant some piece of music for the choir. But in the next instant, I realized that she expected the National Anthem, a piece of music I had intentionally left out of the liturgy, replacing it with my English lady friend's favorite hymn. I asked her to wait until everyone had cleared the line and I'd explain it to her. But she left. There were more such conversations. Some people were angry at my peace-mongering sermons. Some imagined that I cared more for the terrorists who had inflicted a wound in our national mythology than I cared for those who died. As a result, some people left the church, never to return. The lesson I learned in the months after September 11, 2001, is that the hardest thing is rejecting the temptation to bend away from the hope of the Resurrection and toward the kind of nationalism that makes people feel better.

You may know this situation as well as I do. Something terrible happens in our civic life, and we have to plan what to do and say the following Sunday. You recognize that the life that we had shared before is changed. Depending on the circumstances, what the liturgy requires may need to shift to lament, or reconciliation, or forgiveness, and you only have a few precious days or hours to reimagine the liturgy. But, regardless of the circumstances, one phenomenon links all tragedies: we have to acknowledge that the life we share can never be the same again. And no matter how much we try and pretend that we can move along in life as if nothing has happened, we have to craft the liturgy to speak to the tragic moment. Otherwise, it is easy to assume that the church's prayer is ignorant or irrelevant. And the temptation is always to replace the deep healing that comes in the hope of the Resurrection with something short-acting, like nationalism, or liberal political analysis, or queer theory, or antiquarianism, just to name a few of my personal temptations.

The liturgy is the place where we come to encounter God in the living body of Christ. In the context of this body, what we experience is the power of the Resurrection. Just as surely as the burial office is based on the wisdom that "Easter is coming," so the liturgies we craft in times of civic tragedy must be grounded in the Resurrection. This is the source of our wisdom as Christian people. As the hymn "God of Grace and God of Glory" tells us, the liturgy gives us courage and power "for the living of these days." The power of the liturgy is to provide us with a vision of hope that sustains us. This power is not just for those inside the church. We go from the liturgy into the world to share the vision of hope we find in the Resurrection. The liturgy offers us comfort and makes us strong; it is our nursery and our gym. And if we cannot learn to worship together in a Christ-like manner after a civic tragedy, then we have very little likelihood of seeing more of God in the world outside of the church's walls. We come to the liturgy to experience, learn, and practice hope; to live the life of the Resurrection. And if the liturgy doesn't center our lives in the peace of Christ, then our lives will be a torment. At times of civic tragedy, we must learn how to disrupt the prayer book for the sake of Christ's peace.

Despite the perceived sense that liturgy for civic crisis is an occasion to express political ideology, the liturgy must be grounded in the triune God. It's simply not acceptable for nationalism to take the place of the Resurrection. Consider the liturgy following the attacks of September 11 at the Cathedral Church of St. Peter and St. Paul in Washington, D.C. Among the speakers was President George W. Bush, who said from the pulpit, "Just three days removed from these events, Americans do not yet have the distance of history. But our responsibility to history is already clear: to answer these attacks and rid the world of evil."[6] It was

---

6. George W. Bush, "President's Remarks at National Day of Prayer and Remembrance," The White House, September 14, 2001, *https://georgewbush-whitehouse.archives.gov/news/releases/2001/09/20010914-2.html*, accessed April 20, 2020.

a politically and psychologically appealing statement for many. But any statement that stokes the flames of vengeance is the very antithesis of the gospel. The liturgy at the Washington Cathedral serves as a cautionary tale for churches that offer liturgies in times of crisis. When we plan liturgies for civic tragedies, we have to recognize that in the dialectic between nation and church, the gospel must always have the final word. In civic tragedy, we must present the fullness of the gospel to the people who come to pray. Otherwise, our worship is just a spiritual pep rally.

Death, Justice, and Forgiveness

Something must die so that forgiveness can be manifest in the liturgy. Perhaps it is the understanding that we've always nurtured: that forgiveness is only available to those who are penitent. This happens over and over in the liturgy. As Rick Fabian makes clear in his recent volume, making our forgiveness dependent on our repentance is the complete inversion of the gospel's teaching.[7] The liturgy must die to the notion that God is only interested in penitents when it comes to forgiveness. Otherwise, we are in danger of withholding forgiveness from those who injure us. When we hold on to conditional forgiveness, it is easy to mistake justice with vengeance. One of the readings in St. Gregory's Ash Wednesday liturgy comes from the seventh-century theologian Isaac of Nineveh. Isaac writes in his *Ascetic Treatises 60*:

> Do not say God is just. David may call God just and fair, but God's own Son, Jesus, has revealed to us that above all, God is good and kind to the ungrateful and the wicked. It is not someone we might doubt who has told us this, but God's own Son himself. Where is God's justice? Here, in the fact that we were sinners, and Christ died for us.[8]

---

7. Richard Fabian, *Signs of Life: Worship for a Just and Loving People; a Treatise in Eleven Parts* (New York: Church Publishing, 2019), 146–50.

8. Isaac of Nineveh, in Oliver Clement, *Roots of Christian Mysticism* (Hyde Park, NY: New City Press, 1996), 306.

Every year, when I hear this reading, it throws me for a loop; almost no other place in my life dares to speak this truth about justice. Many times, the liturgy presses so firmly into justice that God's mercy and forgiveness are all but absent. Then I find that the liturgy leaves me wanting more justice instead of forgiveness. And, as Isaac reminds me every Ash Wednesday, I'm a sinner. In my sinfulness, I miss out on the fact that my thirst for justice puts me in a tense relationship with forgiveness. I recognize that forgiveness can't take the place of justice, and justice doesn't assure forgiveness. Justice and forgiveness often strive in different directions. Justice wants an exchange to correct the imbalances in life. Forgiveness recognizes that these imbalances cannot always be set right. Ultimately, forgiveness insists that the only exchange that matters is love.

If you've ever wondered what the gospel's definition of "love" is, you'll get as close to the real power of love if you remember that the crown of Jesus's teaching in Luke's gospel tells his followers to love their enemies (Luke 6:27–49). And to eliminate any chance of blurring or metaphorizing this, Jesus insists that to love is to do good, to bless, and to pray for enemies. Jesus isn't teaching us how to have better relationships with our partners or spouses or children. He's not teaching us about healthy family relationships or ethical business relationships. He's not giving us a list of "top ten tips for tip top Christians." In the Gospel of Luke, the only teaching about love has to do with loving our enemies. This teaching is simply breathtaking to me.

When we speak of justice in the liturgy, it must always be in the context of love and forgiveness. The theme of justice in the liturgy cannot "other-ize" or demean those whom we believe have injured us, our enemies, and those who seek our harm. Jesus's teaching makes it clear that enemies are those for whom we pray, not despite the fact that they hate us, curse us, and abuse us, but because they do so. We pray for our enemies as the most Christlike way of imagining justice in the liturgy. The command to love our enemies isn't about an affective sense of love; it is entirely about our actions with our enemies. When Jesus commands his disciples to love their enemies, he doesn't have in mind our contemporary insistence that love is an inner, emotional state. For Jesus, love consists of what you do for another. Jesus's teaching on love means that we enact love as we are doing good for another person. You may not have any affection for the other person and still love the person. This is the context in which justice must be imagined in the liturgy.

One of the reasons that I love the gospel teaching about love is that it depersonalizes my decision to love. The gospel frees me to love by separating love from affect, at least in terms of loving our enemies. I am free to act out of love for people I don't even like. That's something like unconditional love. In the same way, forgiveness is always unconditional. If it isn't, then it isn't forgiveness. If forgiveness comes with conditions, then I'm still chained up in a kind of cage match with my enemy. Forgiving enemies can be stone cold and hard-edged, but it has to be unconditional. Otherwise, it's just about fairness. And the forgiveness we enact in the liturgy is far from fair.

The art of disruption requires us to admit that God's forgiveness means forgiving others without condition. Unconditional forgiveness is the only thing that ultimately releases us from injury, rage, and the bloodthirst that comes with seeking vengeance. We must die to the notion that we don't have to forgive our enemies so that we can become something new. The simplest definition of forgiveness that I've got is this: I refuse to be defined by the violence done to me. When I forgive the one who has hurt me, I am free. I am the recipient of mercy just as surely as I have shown mercy to the one who harms me. I no longer have to suffer the consequences of all my anger. I don't have to be the kind of person who is perpetually defined by being head over heels in hate. Freely forgiving means that we are free and living in the Resurrection.

We need something more than vengeance to stir our hearts in the liturgy. We need much more than justice to keep our lives in balance. The liturgy asks us to forgive others because the liturgy wants worshippers to act like God acts, which is to forgive.

The liturgy reminds us that we have to make a practice of forgiveness for the rest of our lives. The liturgy means for us to do this together. If we are going to act as God acts, we have to be in the company of others who struggle to be real, to forgive, and to love enemies.

All of us share the same vocation: to become as God is, which is the purpose of the liturgy. The commandment to forgive is meant by God to make us truly, eternally alive. I want to understand more and more what God's forgiveness means. I want to live in a way that I am genuinely, unconditionally free. I want to love others not because they are necessarily loveable, but because I am good at loving. I want to experience this love, and learn about this love, and practice this love with everyone who is in the household of God, and outside of it too. This is how we go into the world empowered by God's Spirit to change the world with the power of forgiveness. We get to turn to God's mercy and be transformed by it. We get to lose our rights and the privilege of our grievances. And in their place, we get nothing but mercy to give to each other and the world.

How Could God Let This Happen?

When we are faced with death, either our own or the deaths of our beloved or the deaths of the uncounted thousands who die violently every year, we want answers. So many times people have asked me, "How could God let this happen?" My response is usually theological, talking about God's allowance of freedom and the suffering that may come from human misuse of freedom. The truth is, I am always challenged by this question. It is easy to ask, and impossible to answer, and invites all sorts of shadows to creep into our souls. The place where God lives in me, in you, in the universe around us, is a mystery. Any answer that is a rational attempt to make sense out of a mystery will give cold comfort.

I don't know how to talk rationally about death and resurrection. I don't know how to avoid the trap of believing I can, with my mind alone, make sense out of God's place in our lives. What

I can say is that God does not desire the death of any person. What I can say is that God longs for nothing more than grace and mercy and peace to fill creation. God does not desire the death of anyone. Yet, throughout human history, the death of well-loved children of God has occurred, and it has altered human life and changed the course of events for generations. And it has never, ever been God's will.

We are creatures of God who can make choices. The world is filled with random events that do not have the capacity to care for how we respond to them. The rain will fall where it will fall, and if you are standing in the rain, you will get wet. And although we try to protect ourselves from these random events, we cannot control them. All that we can do is show up and look for signs of the Resurrection. We can act like our foremothers in the faith, those brave, first witnesses of the Resurrection who despite their fear told what they had seen. What we can do is build our liturgy on the foundation of God's love, patterning our work on the example of Jesus's work, rejoicing in the power of his Resurrection. He lived in a world that was similarly shot through with violence. Although it was not broadcast instantaneously around the world, giving every person easy access to scenes of unimaginable suffering and violence was real and omnipresent to Jesus. And it was in this world that he acted to break the back of violence and institute a new way of living. It was in his great sacrifice of love on the cross that he released within us the power to love one another as he loved, forgive one another as he forgave, and live in the power of his Resurrection.

When Jesus poured out his life for us on the cross, he prayed for God's forgiveness to be poured out for all people. He did this for a reason contained in a prayer. This prayer is an invitation to those of us who struggle to look death in the face and strive to make the Resurrection known in our liturgies. The prayer was left by an unknown prisoner in the concentration camp at Ravensbrück during the Shoah. He wrote the words shortly before going into the chambers of death and destruction at that place, and left them on the body of a dead child:

O Lord, remember not only the men and women of good will but also those of ill will. But do not remember all the suffering they have inflicted on us; remember the fruits we have bought, thanks to this suffering—our comradeship, our loyalty, our humility, our courage, our generosity, the greatness of heart which has grown out of all this, and when they come to judgment let all the fruits which we have borne be their forgiveness.[9]

This is what I'm learning about death and resurrection in the liturgy . . .

Hope is born in us when we admit our fear and cling to the Resurrection.

There are only two seasons of the church year: *Easter* and *Easter is coming.*

Our desire to touch brings healing to the dying.

The hope of the Resurrection must always surpass the call of nationalism.

The liturgy cannot talk about justice without unconditional forgiveness.

People need a place to gather when life is unbearably hard.

How have you experienced death and resurrection in the liturgy?

---

9. Caroline J. Simon, "Which Way to Forgiveness?" in *Christian Reflection: A Series in Faith and Ethics*, ed. Robert B. Kruschwitz (Waco, TX: The Center for Christian Ethics at Baylor, 2001), 85.

CHAPTER 6

Beauty, Buildings, and Liturgy

The Image of the Invisible God

I began looking for beauty in church buildings at Bering Drive Church of Christ, the congregation into which I was born. We met in a building that was completed in the early 1960s. If you've spent any time in twentieth-century Christianity, you would recognize my childhood church building. At one end were big, clear glass windows, and at the other end was a wall covered in a random arrangement of wooden slats and blocks all pointing upward. At the center of this wall, behind a screen of slats and blocks, was the baptistry, a tank of water for immersion.

The high-pitched ceiling was wood, and laminated wooden beams arched from the floor to the pinnacle of the building, the arches marching down the length of the room. On either side of the front wall were smaller white brick walls set out from the back about ten feet; in front of one was a pulpit, and in front of the other was a podium. At the center was a pale wooden communion table. There were no crosses, no flowers, and no candles, just a gooseneck microphone stand in the middle of the holy table.

When I was a child, I would frequently get bored during the service. My family attended faithfully, and I would sit next to my mother, who provided a buffer between my brother and me. When I would fidget, she would hand me a deposit slip from her checkbook or the insert from the worship leaflet to use for drawing. I would draw during the spoken parts of the service, sometimes pausing to sing one of the hymns I liked. The only time that my mother wouldn't let me draw was during communion, which we celebrated every Sunday. Then I had to put down my paper and pay attention. I asked my mother what I was supposed to do during communion; invariably she would reply, "Think about Jesus." And I would think about Jesus. But I would also look at the wall in front of me, the wooden slats and white brick. If my family sat close enough to the front, I could see that the white bricks weren't a solid color but had texture and pattern. If communion went on for too long, or if I ran out of things to draw, I would look closely at the texture and pattern of the bricks and imagine that there were images in them. The mottled texture of the bricks showed me faces and snow scenes, mountains, and forests; sometimes, I even saw scenes that included Jesus. This is how I began to notice the building of the church, by using my imagination to see what the building didn't intend to show.

My earliest memories were visual. The first thing I recall was the sky in its beautiful blueness. When I think of my early childhood, it's always like watching a movie on a screen. The images outside of me somehow became images inside of me. In my childhood, I would see things that weren't obvious to other people: as with the white bricks in my childhood church, I would look at the woodgrain in the paneling at my home and see faces, and imagine that these faces had personalities. So my relationship to beauty and meaning in the world is deep and lifelong. When I look at the world, I am seeking beauty, which is another way of seeking after God. This is where I begin to imagine the space for the liturgy and how to hack the space for the liturgy: looking for beauty, which is always a revelation of God.

Beauty and Evangelism

In my life, I have spent thousands of hours in church buildings, just looking. I look at the architecture and the art, the spaces for children, and the notice board—memorial plaques whose history nobody can remember. I look at church buildings that I visit and my own in San Francisco. I notice where the paint needs touching up and when the icons need to be changed. Often I do this when my mind wanders during a sermon; I always do this when I enter the building for the first time. Almost ten years ago I was talking to a parishioner, my friend Elizabeth, about her sense of our building. "On occasion, I try to look at our church as a stranger would see it," she said. "Does that look right? Does it look balanced? Is there something uneven there? Is it jarring?" Elizabeth understood that the way the building looks matters; paying attention to beauty is a spiritual practice. And it is always an evangelistic act; we pay attention to beauty in the building for the sake of those who haven't found their way in yet.

Anyone who walks into a church building gets a sense of its meaning and whether or not it is a space that welcomes them. People experience beauty either consciously or unconsciously because there is an insistent quality to beauty. The insistence of beauty raises questions about my identity as I come to worship. If the space is huge, dark, and mysterious, I may know myself as small, subject, and vulnerable. If the space is casual and disorganized, I may know myself as critical, aloof, and invulnerable. If I walk into a church building and find that the liturgy is in the side chapel, I wonder why I am being seated in coach instead of first class. If the nave was designed to hold five hundred people and there are twenty-five spread throughout the room, I wonder if group interaction is discouraged. There are as many experiences of church buildings as there are people who come into them. People come into church buildings seeking to encounter God, revealed in beauty.

Beauty is experienced differently by different people. There isn't a single standard for beauty. Some people prefer beauty that is minimal, and some like maximal beauty. Some people want to be surrounded by a blur of color, and some want monochrome. Beauty is distinct from these preferences; beauty and taste are two different things. Too often, churches confuse beauty and taste, and consequently accept or reject art and the objects we use in worship.

From time to time, people tell me that the art at St. Gregory's seems self-consciously over the top. Art that is merely attractive is not our goal. We strive for beauty that tells us more about God. We use many objects to both adorn the church building and enhance the liturgy. Some of these are made by members, and some come from other parts of the world. We strive to use art and objects to show that beauty is not bound by any one culture, religion, or era. By displaying this art and using these objects in the liturgy, we are showing that the love of God is not limited by culture, religion, or era. This art may not be to everyone's taste, but the only thing that is ugly is what separates us from God and each other. The solution to ugliness is the same as the solution to sin: the redemptive love of God.

People are hungry for beauty. If we are cut off from beauty, the capacity to imagine the world as God knows it is diminished. When the church ignores beauty, it is easy to forget that in the beginning, God looked at the creation and called it good. Beauty is not an option for us; it is where we meet God. Beauty is the first word that speaks to people in the liturgy. Before the gospel is proclaimed or the sacraments are shared, people know God in the encounter with beauty. When we do not privilege beauty in our buildings, we veil the revelation of God, impoverishing the people of God.

Beauty is complex and pluralistic; it makes itself known through all of our senses. When people enter the church building, beauty approaches them in a full range of sensory experience—not only how the room looks, but what it smells like, what sounds are present, how the atmosphere of the room presses against their skin, even the way taste is evoked if there is coffee nearby. And, as my friend Elizabeth understood, visitors notice things that regular attendees may not: the orderliness or messiness of the children's space, the notices posted in the narthex that are weeks or months old, the loud hum of the HVAC system. People are attuned to the beauty that is expressed not only in the beautiful objects the building contains, but the scale and harmony of the room's design.

People, Buildings, and Liturgy

People often come to St. Gregory's during the week and ask to look inside the building. I take them up to the front doors and explain the burning bush mosaic that greets them and its inscription: "All that is prays to you." I open the carved wooden doors and follow them in. People step in and always look up at the massive icon of dancing saints on the walls of the rotunda. They step further into the building and stand looking, and I say, "you really can't appreciate the building unless you're here for worship. It doesn't make sense unless you see how people occupy it."

Louis Weil, professor emeritus of liturgics at the Church Divinity School of the Pacific, famously said, "Don't argue with the building, the building always wins."[1] Weil meant that the way a church building is ordered will override whatever is *said* about theology in the space. Still, liturgists and worship leaders continue to argue with their buildings. No matter what they intend, if the altar is far removed from the people, a liturgy that emphasizes the whole priestly people will seem phony. If the pews have been replaced with chairs arranged in a semicircle, a liturgy that wants people to focus on a single sacred point will fall flat. Congregations have buildings that liturgy planners ignore, hoping that worship will somehow fit into the space; it doesn't always work. Then the building wins the argument, and the liturgy loses. And when the liturgy loses, so do the people.

The variable that has the power to shift the argument between the building and the liturgy is the people who come to worship. Before we design a liturgy or imagine how it will be staged in a church building, we have to imagine how people will occupy the space. The liturgy is more than a text, and the building more than a pretty place. Without people, church buildings are incomplete. We have to get curious about the people who come to worship and how we use the buildings where they gather. Then we have to plan the liturgy based on how people will use the building. Even then there can be a disconnect between the plans we make and the experience of worship.

The first time I worshipped in a congregation of the Episcopal Church, it was in a cathedral building. In 1983, I was a college student in Memphis, Tennessee. On a winter morning, I stumbled,

---

1. John Ander Runkle, *Searching for Sacred Space: Essays on Architecture and Liturgical Design in the Episcopal Church* (New York: Church Publishing, 2002), 152.

slightly bleary from my late Saturday night, into St. Mary's Episcopal Cathedral. Established in 1858, it is one of the first cathedrals in the Episcopal Church; the current building was completed in 1926. I think the liturgy was a Rite One Morning Prayer. I remember the cool efficiency with which the service progressed and how the building perfectly contained the liturgy. In front of a limestone reredos and altar was a small chancel with choir stalls facing each other. Three steps down were dark brown pews, carved with gothic finials at the ends. The choir sat in their seats, and the congregation sat in their places where we listened and occasionally responded. We stood to sing, sat to listen, and knelt to pray. The space was designed for the passive reception of the liturgy; there was no argument between the liturgy and the building. But the people, at least me, didn't seem to be of much concern to the liturgy.

During the service, I felt fidgety. The rows of pews were too tightly packed together, and the varnished wood felt slightly sticky. The building made me feel small and disconnected. It wasn't just the way that the choir sat in the front, the preacher stood in a high pulpit, and we all sat below facing the same direction. It seemed to me that the space of the cathedral was designed to shape people's self-understanding.

The shape of the liturgy, and the building, forms people's imaginations. Sometimes this shape teaches people that they are to be still and receive whatever is offered to them. It can seem like make-believe. Most of life privileges questioning and engagement; many church buildings are designed to keep people's mouths shut and bodies still. Liturgy as performance puts people into space that emphasizes the distinction between audience and performer. This was my first experience at St. Mary's Cathedral.

Twenty-five years later, I returned to the same cathedral to join in a conversation with a large group of church leaders called the Great Emergence Event. The gathering was a combination of worship and workshops, discussions, and debates about the changing nature of the church in the twenty-first century. Among the featured leaders of the event was Phyllis Tickle, the elder sister of what was then called "The Emerging Church."

Organizers of the event held the worship and plenary sessions in the cathedral. The experience was nothing like what I had experienced a quarter-century before. Although the arrangement of the room was still dark pews and choir stalls, the way people used the room challenged the design of the building. As the gathering pressed the enveloping shell of stained glass and limestone, the building made less and less sense.

There was little attention to beauty in the gathering. The cathedral was nothing more than a meeting room. Like my first experience of worship there, this event also included a performance-oriented style of worship: the people at the front talked and sang, and the audience received what was delivered. As I sat and listened, I felt that same fidgety sense of wanting to do something.

I wondered about the choice to abandon the high pulpit for a bar stool in the middle of the chancel. The pulpit would have been a more accessible place to see and hear the speakers; the bar stool communicated availability while keeping the speakers remote. There was a tangle of mics and music stands and what seemed like miles of cables haphazardly lying on the chancel floor. Ignoring the cathedral's design denied its beauty. Instead of accentuating our humanity, the messy arrangement communicated that human bodies didn't matter that much and beauty was optional.

Seven years after this, I found myself, once again, at St. Mary's Cathedral for the funeral of my friend Phyllis Tickle. I loved Phyllis and respected her as a wisdom figure in the church. And although her death was a relief from suffering and rebirth into eternal life, it was a sad day. It was a beautiful liturgy that balanced the formality of my first visit and the messiness of my previous visit. The choir sang robustly, and the bishop's sermon was heartfelt. There was a real sense of a community together at prayer, coming to grieve a friend's death; the hope and power of the Resurrection were present. The building was packed with people from across the country. Although I felt the same energetic presence as I had at the earlier gathering of emergent church leaders, the traditional design of the building was embraced.

I noticed something more about the space. It was a bright, fall day; the stained-glass windows blazed with color. Maybe it was because of the brightness of the light that day or because of the deep feeling that attended me, but the room was full of energy. I didn't notice the kind of damp chill I had experienced decades before. The building held the congregation, offering its beauty as another source of comfort. It was as if people's hope in the Resurrection, love of Phyllis, and hunger for beauty all fit together in the space.

There were flowers in abundance. People filled the room. The liturgy comforted us. Strangers had become friends, and the losses of the past no longer could harm. The room was filled with tears and laughter, and wave after wave of people expressing their love. All of them were God's beloved. All of them were knit together into a community because of the Resurrection.

The Revelation of Beauty

Beauty reveals God because God is beautiful. The beauty of God is revealed in an infinite number of ways. When we come together in prayer, God's beauty is revealed in the words and actions of the liturgy, in the physical space for worship, and in the presence of each person who comes to pray. Beauty is all around us when we gather, even when our desire for it is numbed. But our desire is the key to the experience of beauty; all we have to do to welcome beauty is desire it. The problem is that we don't always trust the wisdom of our desire, so we desire beauty too little. We tamp down our desire for beauty and instead desire something less: our privilege or rights or personal comfort. None of these are necessarily unworthy goals, but none of these are enough to fulfill our desire; God is the one who is great enough to warrant our desire. And God is beautiful.

As we press more and more into our desire for God, we discover more of the beauty of God. In our desire for God, more of the divine presence is revealed to us. As God's presence fills more and more of our lives, we discover that the whole point of life is to become as God is—loving, generous, merciful, and beautiful. The revelation of God makes us beautiful and urges our desire forward to experience more of God's presence. Our desire is like our hunger; it cannot be satisfied without taking into ourselves what comes from outside us. The only satisfaction comes as we are filled with God's presence, which is always beautiful. God comes to us in beauty so that we may reflect beauty in the world that God loves. And then, as we encounter God's beauty in the world, we see more of God.

Because God is revealed as beauty, we cannot make beauty optional in the words and actions of the liturgy or the physical space for worship. We must be ready to welcome the beauty that comes in the presence of each person who comes to pray. The beauty of the liturgy challenges the banality that too often fills our lives and helps us to see that we too are beautiful. As we are enriched by the liturgy, taking into the world the grace we receive, we can see more beauty in the world. The whole world is filled with this promise; all we have to do is take notice.

This kind of mindfulness is where we can begin the work of justice in the world; it makes us ready to strive for what is fair. As Elaine Scarry notes, beauty helps us pay attention to justice.[2] The things that make beauty evident to us, things like harmony, balance, symmetry, and ultimately fairness, touch us, changing the ways that we are in the world. Approaching beauty is like turning on a light switch: it makes what is right in front of us suddenly, obviously apparent. The grace of the liturgy has the power to turn on this light switch. As we go forth into the world, we go transformed to welcome the encounter with justice and beauty.

The process of transformation is generative. When we see beauty, it recalls other experiences of beauty in our lives. In the same way, when we act for the sake of justice, we are more finely tuned to justice as we encounter it in our lives. Beauty and justice enliven us and show us what is true in the world around us.

---

2. Elaine Scarry, *On Beauty and Being Just* (Princeton, NJ: Princeton University Press, 2001).

This truth then energizes us to strive for what is animating in the world and to share the experience with others. Scarry writes, "Beauty is, then, a compact, or contract between the beautiful being . . . and the perceiver. As the beautiful being confers on the perceiver the gift of life, so the perceiver confers on the beautiful being the gift of life."[3] Beauty destabilizes and creates opportunities to view the world in a new way, as a place where liveliness is the norm instead of the exception.

Early in the pandemic lockdown, I would go by the church building once a week to make sure everything was secure. A sign on the front doors said, "Out of precaution due to COVID-19, St. Gregory's is closed until further notice." I would pick up the mail from the office and check the locks. Then I would go up into the beautiful space where we have gathered for worship since 1995. I had turned off the furnace, so the room was colder than usual. The hangings were made from *bògòlanfini*—Malian mud cloth—that we use in the season of Lent. Everything looked the way it did when we had our final liturgy before we went online for worship.

On the last Sunday that we were able to gather and celebrate the eucharist, our bishop, Marc Andrus, had instructed us not to share the chalice. Like all of his pastoral directions, his words were gentle and humane, an effort to protect the weakest members of our community from infection. During the liturgy that Sunday, I decided that if the people couldn't share the chalice, it would be best if the presider didn't either. I placed a single chalice on the altar and a clear cruet of wine. Before I began the Great Thanksgiving, I said, "This chalice is empty today because we cannot share it. But the wine is here. We will ask God's blessing on it and then save it until we can gather here and share it." At the end of the liturgy, I placed the consecrated wine in our ambry, a Japanese shrine shaped like a house.

Every time that I would go to the church building during the lockdown, I would stop and reverence the presence of Christ in the wine we had reserved. Sometimes I would weep; other times I

---

3. Ibid., 90.

would not. And I would pray that the grace of the eucharist would be spiritually available to our community. Surrounded by so much beauty, my prayer was as much for what I knew of my parishioners' needs as it was for my fear in not knowing what would come. But what I remember most about those moments of prayer was the presence of the dancing saints icon on the walls above me—the visual reminder of the unseen cloud of witnesses that accompanies us whether we are together or apart. Beauty holds us; it is our warrant that God is with us.

The Sacred and the Profane

Luke's gospel tells a story about the relationship between sacred space, prayer, and justice. The building in which this familiar story is staged was designed according to a rule that made it essential to separate the sacred and the profane. "Two men went up to the temple to pray, one a Pharisee, the other a tax collector. . . . The tax collector stood some distance away, not daring even to raise his eyes to heaven; but he beat his breast and said, 'God, be merciful to me, a sinner'" (cf. Luke 18:10–14).

The temple in Jerusalem, like all sacred buildings in the ancient world, was a space that maintained different areas of sanctity. It was really more than just a single building; there was a series of courtyards and colonnades that surrounded the temple. The outermost court of the temple was for everyone; we know it as the court of the Gentiles, but every Judean at the time would have defined Gentiles as "people who are not us." Then there was the court of women, the area where women who were members of the covenant could gather. Then there was the court of Israel, the place for men in the covenant. Then there was the building of the temple, the space for the priestly caste to do their business. Then there were the divisions of the temple itself, the holy place for the aristocratic, priestly caste and the holy of holies, the place where the high priest would enter just once a year to offer sacrifice. These concentric rings of sanctity were not only to keep people separate; they were designed to keep people in a relative relationship to God: the closer you could get to the holy of holies, the more sacred was your status.

The parable of the Pharisee and the tax collector has this kind of division in mind. It begins with the premise that beauty and justice divide between holiness and commonness. In the course of the parable, the two characters embrace this division. One rejoices in his privilege, and the other bewails his sin. The Pharisee and the tax collector pray in ways that are defined by place, posture, gesture, and language.

They are together, praying in the court of Israel. The Pharisee draws as near as he can to the sacred center, his face turned toward the holy of holies, and talks to himself about his great relationship to God. The tax collector, on the other hand, stands far off, downcast, striking his chest and asking God to have mercy on him. Each one occupies the sacred space and performs his prayer in a way that defines his relationship to God.

Just as the temple complex was an architecture that defined the pure and the impure in space, these two men are establishing their relationship to God in space and gesture and word. But there is a relationship between the two men. And in a way that is confirmed over and over in my experience, the more powerful defines the relationship. The thing that relates them is the Pharisee's utter contempt for the tax collector.

Sadly, this ancient ordering of sacred space is reflected in many church buildings, and often this classical ordering is superficially beautiful. The notion that far away, in some even more beautiful space, God is pleased to dwell inaccessibly, is familiar. It is a message drilled into us every day by those who may believe that God's holiness is necessarily removed from us. Ordering church buildings like the temple in Jerusalem as a set of concentric zones of sanctity makes sense unless you read the gospels, where you find a different story. What constitutes sanctity in the gospels is always the unexpected, the unimagined, and the marginal. The sacred space in the gospel is occupied by desperate housewives seeking lost coins and unethical managers making side deals with tree-climbing rejects and crucified criminals. The gospel tells us that the division between the sacred and the profane is a construct of human sinfulness.

St. Gregory's church building, unlike a lot of sacred buildings today, has no space that defines the sacred against the profane, the elite against the common. The whole space is sacred, just as the entire world is sacred. The altar-table sits on the same level as the people who draw near to receive God's love in bread and wine. And we sit facing each other for the liturgy of the word. We do this to see the original icon of God: the human person who is facing you. We are the icon because that is where it has pleased God to be known. We are that icon because God desires to share through us the mercy and love that God has for everyone.

Beauty that levels the distinction between the sacred and the common is the best goal for the spaces where we celebrate the liturgy. When we work against the division between the holy and the common, our eyes are opened to see the most faithful revelation of God's beauty. And when we recognize that God's beauty is revealed everywhere that God is pleased to dwell, our eyes are opened to see God at work in the places we too often imagine God's absence. Then we can see that God's beauty is not restricted by suffering or weakness. In her book on Gregory of Nyssa, Natalie Carnes notes that the power of such beauty is found as it challenges our easy assimilation to cruelty and sloth.[4] She continues, "For Gregory, Christ is present in the poor, hungry, diseased, and bestialized, how the transcendent beauty of God, the Beauty that beckons us ever-onward, is deeply intertwined with the ugliness of this world."[5]

Strangers Seeking Beauty

The word that best describes Christians is "amateurs" from the Latin root *amare*, to love. The church is a community of amateurs,

---

4. Natalie Carnes, *Beauty: A Theological Engagement with Gregory of Nyssa* (Eugene, OR: Cascade Books, 2014), Kindle Edition, Loc. 96.

5. Ibid., Loc. 184.

of those who love and act out of love. We are born with a desire for beauty. We seek beauty because of the love that God plants in our hearts. Because of this, the people who come to the liturgy have a stake in beauty, both in beholding it and creating it. The liturgy and the places where we worship are where people can experiment and test out new ways of approaching beauty, worship, learning, relationships, and the work God is putting before them. Seeking beauty is our souls' vocation, whether we acknowledge Christ's Lordship or not.

People come to church buildings seeking beauty. The beauty of the "church's house" includes more than superficial interior decoration. The beauty of a church building comes from its truth, its authenticity, and its generosity. A church building is beautiful because it is unabashedly holy, but doesn't segregate the sacred from the common. Church buildings are beautiful because they welcome ordinary human beings—not only church members— into them. Church buildings are beautiful in as far as they provide a space for people to encounter extraordinary experience. The sacred enclosure for the liturgy is genuinely holy as we open it to the world, to amateurs and experts alike.

According to a 2012 study, researchers found that 88 percent of the people who visited English cathedrals did so because they got a sense of the sacred from the building.[6] It did not matter whether respondents called themselves Christians or not. The research also found that beauty, in the architecture, art, or music, was a point of spiritual connection for 35 percent of non-church attenders.[7] These findings suggest that the experience of beauty isn't dependent on people's religious affiliation; beauty reveals God whether you believe in God or not.

In terms of evangelism, this is profoundly important. Instead of putting up barriers to people who are seeking spiritual connection by keeping our buildings locked up, we have an opportunity

---

6. Theos and the Grubb Institute, *Spiritual Capital: The Present and Future of English Cathedrals* (London: Theos and the Grubb Institute, 2012), 29.

7. Ibid., 31.

to reach out to them just by opening our doors, freely sharing their beauty with anyone who seeks it. These findings are personally significant to me.

My husband Grant is an agnostic. He comes once a year to St. Gregory's, for the Christmas Eve pageant service, but he doesn't have the kind of personal faith that draws him to the liturgy, to prayer, or to the sacraments. What he does know is beauty. He has a clear understanding of aesthetics and definite opinions about what is visually pleasing. He is a man who delights in beauty wherever he encounters it, in high culture and pop culture, in nature and in cities, in architecture, even in typography.

Grant and I like to travel together. We've been to Europe a few times in the twenty years of our relationship. Wherever we go, we visit church buildings. We've been to St. Peter's Basilica in Rome, Notre Dame in Paris, and Westminster Abbey in London. And we've been to tiny chapels, village churches, and the archeological remains of church buildings. In these buildings, Grant is captivated by beauty. Although he might not name it in religious terms, he gains that sense of spiritual reality that permeates sacred space.

We stumbled onto a church in Paris after Christmas one year. We stepped inside to see the building and immediately heard singing; a choir of young people was practicing for a holiday concert. The acoustics of the room were perfect. The building itself was an ornate, over-the-top baroque thing. We stood listening to the sound of the singing, looking at the gilded expanse above us. Grant said quietly, "Beautiful. How great that this is here. It's like they're singing just for us." When we visit church buildings, my agnostic husband and I share the same spiritual experience of encountering beauty.

Church buildings are lively spaces where people gather. Some come to church so that they can rehearse the axial moments of their lives. Some come because their faith draws them Sunday by Sunday to encounter God. Some, like Grant, come because they love beauty and find that it fills their hearts with joy. Church buildings are spaces of memory and hope; they are thin spaces where the ordinary busyness of life is briefly overwhelmed by the presence of God. Church buildings are like gifts waiting to be opened; they invite us to encounter the surprising quality of beauty that we haven't expected to see.

We do a disservice when we consider our church buildings as private places. Church buildings are meeting places of human and divine longing. For both the faithful and the skeptical, they are places to encounter the eternal, discovered in the presence of beauty. All this can happen when we recognize that church buildings are public spaces, not private enclaves of privilege. When we open the doors and welcome people to come into the building, they have the hope of encountering something that is greater than they are. Not everyone wants to participate in the liturgy. Sometimes people look into church buildings to find silence, or a work of art, or just a chance to catch their breath in the course of a busy day. There are as many different opportunities for people to engage beauty as there are church buildings.

Congregations can prepare their buildings to welcome people with hospitality and the invitation to encounter beauty in ritual ways. Some people may walk in off the street to light a candle even though they may have no idea of the relationship between candle lighting and prayer. Some may come in and kneel quietly at the altar even though they wouldn't consider eucharistic fellowship. The desire of unchurched people is all that they need to share in ritual action. In each of these moments, we can generously invite the encounter with beauty. We can allow people to wander, to explore, and to pray alone. We can establish different centers of sacred encounter. The side chapel, the labyrinth, the font are all places where we can welcome people who may call themselves "spiritual but not religious."

I witness these people almost every time I visit Grace Cathedral in San Francisco. I will come to Grace for a diocesan liturgy or the occasional evensong, and see these "spiritual tourists" shyly walking around the perimeter of the room. I notice that the official liturgy happening ten feet away from them is not what is most compelling for many of them. For a spiritual tourist, simply walking and looking is the goal. Often, while the diocesan liturgy is taking place, I notice these spiritual tourists quietly kneeling to the side or lighting a candle. A spiritual tourist may not come expecting to have any particular experience of God, but they are open to the invitation of spiritual connection, however it comes.

Church buildings are obviously more than museums, places where people wander mindlessly looking at the building through their iPhones. We must be ready to engage spiritual tourists so that they can have a more profound experience of the space. We have to be careful not to send the wrong message to people who don't know the meaning of the building or its fixtures. I walked into an English cathedral several years ago, a destination I had looked forward to visiting for years. It was crowded with tourists. I noticed that they had helpfully set up signs at the sacred locations through the building. By one was a placard that read, "The Font: the place of Baptism into the church" with a "do not enter" symbol next to it. The mixed message was laughable; needless to say, I did not attempt to touch the baptismal water it contained.

People continue looking for the beautiful, the real, and the authentic. Simply because they don't know the rules doesn't mean they're uninterested in spiritual connection. We need to welcome spiritual tourists generously and with hospitality, just as Christ welcomes us to his table. This welcome implies both strategic changes and technical fixes.

Strategically, we can begin planning the ways we use our buildings with strangers and visitors as our target audience. This will require congregational leaders to ask tough questions about how much we want strangers to share our buildings and how we can open our boundaries to people who may never join the church. At St. Gregory's, we made the strategic choice to host our weekly food pantry inside of the church building, gathering around the altar in the middle of the rotunda. We welcome people to come and get food in the most beautiful space we have because we trust that their experience of beauty opens them to transformation.

Technically, we must provide resources and opportunities to strangers and visitors who come to our buildings. These may include providing informational brochures, smartphone apps, or people who come to the building to wait for visitors to welcome. Technical fixes may also mean that we have to offer our church buildings for outside groups who want to lead yoga or tai-chi classes. Every other Sunday at St. Gregory's we host an icon painting workshop in the rotunda. We have cards with the dates of the workshops, folding tables, and a storage area for materials. At the end of the Sunday liturgy, we recruit members of the church to set up the tables so that icon painters come into the building already prepared for them to work.

Opening the most beautiful spaces we have for those who come is a spiritual discipline. As the encounter with beauty is the encounter with God, our generous welcome of strangers and visitors is for transformation. The experiences people have in our church buildings are the goal. And we must be grateful for those who visit us, even though they may never come again, join the membership, or make a pledge. Our motivation is reflected in one of our Good Friday prayers: "That as Christ came as a stranger to befriend us, we may learn to welcome those unknown and alien to us."

Bodies in Space

Our bodies matter in worship. How our bodies engage in prayer is of equal importance to the ways our minds engage it. And yet too often worship communicates that our bodies do not matter and that the space in which our bodies worship doesn't either. Yet the Incarnation of Jesus Christ says otherwise. It is in his human body that Jesus redeems us, and our bodies are where we know our redemption. Our bodies, redeemed by God, are holy and intended by God for sacred purposes.

The Apostle Paul writes to the church in Corinth, telling them that they are "God's temple" (1 Corinthians 3:16). Our whole selves are the dwelling place of God's Spirit. In the broader context of his letter to the Corinthians, with all of its concern for the ways our bodies are in holy relationships with each other, Paul intends us to understand that our physical bodies are God's temple. And just to emphasize the significance of our bodies, he concludes, "For God's temple is holy, and you are that temple" (1 Corinthians 3:17). The use of the word "body" throughout 1 Corinthians indicates both our individual bodies and the gathered Body that is Christ's.

The spaces where we gather for worship are gatherings of holy bodies, paradigms of the temple, bearers of God's Holy Spirit. This is why worship is always an incarnational event and our bodies are instruments of prayer. We must pay attention to human bodies and how they occupy the buildings in which we worship. We must attend to how church buildings welcome us as embodied human beings. This is not always an easy practice because we do not always have a healthy relationship with our bodies. Too often it is easier to hate our bodies than it is to love them as the revelation of God that Christ promises us they are.

In my life, I have had an ambivalent relationship with my body. There are plenty of reasons for this relationship: I was a fat kid. I was an uncoordinated kid. I was a young, gay, closeted, introverted, six-and-a-half-foot tall, Evangelical seminarian. But I have learned to love my body. And St. Gregory's—with our practices of embodied prayer—has taught me the value of bodies and their beauty. Disrupting the prayer book shows me how to love my body in its full, God-haunted splendor, knowing it as a source of wisdom and beauty.

Bodies, Beauty, and Liturgy

The wisdom of my body sometimes insists that I pay attention to the world in ways that my mind and emotions do not. When I exert myself, my body's intelligence doesn't let me forget what I've done: sore muscles and tired feet are a standard feature in my experience of the liturgies of Holy Week. And because St. Gregory's changes the arrangement of the room for these liturgies, the opportunities to learn from the wisdom of my body are always there.

Just before Holy Week 2019, I was rearranging the chairs and platforms for the Triduum liturgies. Although we have rollers under the platforms, moving them requires a lot of physical exertion. I should have waited for some helpers to show up, but I get a kind of manic enthusiasm to get things done during Holy Week. I managed to rearrange four of the eight-foot by ten-foot platforms, and about half of the 150 chairs before the rest of the set-up crew arrived.

The next morning I woke up with that familiar muscle soreness and fatigue that doesn't feel precisely bad. It was a reminder that my body is an instrument that still works, although not as smoothly as it did twenty-five years ago. The next day was Saturday before Palm Sunday, and more than twenty people showed up to make the building ready. We have an elaborate way of decorating the building for Palm Sunday. We hang twelve-foot-long palm fronds from ropes and hoist them high above the altar in the middle of the rotunda. The palm branches hang from four of the eight corners of the room, gracefully arching up from the walls to the cupola, with more tall palm branches by each door. We festoon the building in red fabric. We prepare for the lavish breakfast we serve to everyone before the Sunday liturgy.

I spent hours with the Palm Sunday team getting the space ready. I can't tell you how many times I stooped down, or climbed up, or knelt on the concrete floor. We laughed at corny jokes and tried to remember the way we hoisted the palm branches the year before. At noon we took a break for lunch and then set up tables under the arching palm fronds for Palm Sunday breakfast.

I woke up on Sunday morning, rolled out of bed, and immediately my back seized up. The pleasant soreness of the previous day was replaced by the kind of shooting pain that wouldn't let me go. Bodies have their own wisdom.

When we plan the liturgy, we have to attend to the wisdom of our bodies. This is particularly the case in liturgies that ask for more than usual physical engagement. The Palm Sunday liturgy is one of these. Every congregation has its customs when it comes to the procession. Since it is one of the only processional liturgies in the Book of Common Prayer, it's worth looking at the specific rubric related to the palm procession. The prayer book says, "When circumstances permit, the congregation may gather at a place apart from the church, so that all may go into the church in procession."[8]

The Palm Sunday liturgy offers opportunities for a close reading of the rubrics and a generous interpretation of them. What the rubrics say is that the congregation may gather apart from the building and enter the church in procession. But where do we gather first? How do we gather there? How do we get from one place to another? When do we go into the building if we gather outdoors? The ways that we answer these questions may create the liturgy in transformative and lifegiving ways, or they may not. The choices that we make when we read the rubrics matter.

At St. Gregory's, we have our procession halfway through the liturgy. We gather for breakfast in the rotunda, then clean up and begin the liturgy as we usually do. After the sermon and prayers, we leave the building, walking down the street with branches in our hands. We stop outside of the Whole Foods store and bless the palms, first singing the traditional words, "Today the grace of the Holy Spirit has gathered us together, so we all take up our cross and say, blessed is the king who comes in the name of the Lord, hosanna in the highest." We carry our palm branches around the block singing a call and response written by Ben Allaway that our cantor calls out through a red cheerleader megaphone.[9] We continue around the block, generally making a racket and pausing across the street from the million-dollar condos to hear the words of scripture as people lean out the windows and watch. We then return to the church building to share the bread and wine.

The Palm Sunday procession is not a reenactment. We do not carry branches in the streets as a make-believe of the triumphal entry of Jesus into Jerusalem, although it is the gospel reading of that event that informs our action. Instead, the palm procession is a present engagement of human bodies as instruments of prayer.

---

8. Book of Common Prayer, 270.

9. Ben Allaway, "Hosanna Ho," in *Music by Heart: Paperless Songs for Evening Worship: A Collection of Songs from the New Music Project* (New York: Church Publishing, 2008), 132.

The procession is a real event; real people get up and walk in the streets. The value of this kind of liturgy is to publicly confess the power of Christ's passion for anyone who is there to bear witness. The procession is not nostalgic; it is the bold expression as embodied people at prayer.

Nostalgia is a way of acting that seeks comfort in an imagined ideal of the past. Unlike an embodied, processional liturgy, nostalgia is easy to manage. The Palm Sunday procession may be chaotic, it may be unpredictable, it may be a struggle, but it is never make-believe. If the liturgy intends to meet the living God amid the lively people, it can have nothing to do with nostalgia. It pleases God to come to us in our bodies, in our lived experiences. So on Palm Sunday we say, "Blessed is the one who comes in the name of the Lord." And the response is "Hosanna in the highest," not "Let's play make-believe." We claim the peace of God that is always with us, surrounding us, filling us, and redeeming us—doing all this in ourselves, our souls and bodies. We do this every time we take up our palm branches and walk the streets of the city, singing our hope out to any who will listen. And we do this as we trek back to our everyday lives, open and vulnerable to the world around us.

The procession on Palm Sunday in 2019 wasn't easy. My back was killing me. Later, I watched a video that someone had made of the liturgy. The look my face told the story of my physical aches: a kind of grimace behind a fake smile. And still, walking back into the church building at the end of the procession, all of us singing "All glory laud and honor," I forgot the pain for a moment. Looking up at the palms hanging from the ceiling, seeing the gashes of red fabric hanging from crosses, hearing the insistent drumming that accompanied the hymn, my heart was uplifted. And as happens so often in the Holy Week liturgies, tears blurred my vision. There was so much beauty, so much suffering, so much joy.

No matter where you go, the Body of Christ will be your body. And just like an ache in your muscles that refuses to go away, no matter how hard you will it to leave, God's presence won't leave you alone. Any liturgy worth celebrating recognizes that in Christ's suffering and loss, there is the promise of new life and new hope—not a nostalgic trip back over the centuries, but a real and present experience of the God who is. For the God who is, is with us in the places we gather for worship.

———————

This is what I'm learning about beauty, buildings, and the liturgy . . .

Church buildings are another text of the gospel.

People's hunger for beauty reveals God to them.

There must be congruity between the liturgy and
the building.

If we do not privilege beauty in the liturgy, we diminish
the revelation of God.

Sharing the spaces in which we worship is evangelistic.

Our bodies are the best guides for planning the liturgy.

How do you respond physically to beauty, buildings, and the liturgy?

CHAPTER 7

Challenges, Principles, and Liturgy

The Challenge of Disruption

Our house in San Francisco is in the middle of the city, on a busy street across from a row of nearly identical Victorian homes. Ours isn't a large house, but there is enough room for us and our dog, Frankie. A few years ago, we turned the single-car garage into a painting studio for me; my husband Grant calls it my man cave. To me, it is both a creative sanctuary and a workshop. There are cabinets for supplies and an inspiration board where I tack pictures of icons, color samples of tempera paint, notes, and a sweet painting by my three-year old great-niece. In March 2020, it also became my office and livestream studio, where I crafted the liturgy for St. Gregory's and performed it for my congregation online. It is also the place where I learned more about myself as a priest and a person who cares about the liturgy. Were it not for the lockdown enforced in the early days of COVID-19, I would never have understood the deepest meaning of the word disruption and how it applies to the liturgy.

The pandemic disrupted virtually every part of our common life. Indeed, for us who lead people in the liturgy, the disruptions challenged us to reimagine both what the liturgy is and the fundamental meaning of worship. Those days of the pandemic taught me that the art of disruption is more than a technical fix for the church. Instead, it is a strategy to transform a reimagined church in a radically changed world. Before the pandemic we lived with a set of assumptions about the social gathering of God's people at prayer that no longer hold. In this time, after the worst of the pandemic, we have two choices: we can try and return to the former world, or we can admit that we have to understand worship in a new way.

As I sat in my home office/painting study/livestream studio writing the last parts of this book, I had to learn a new way of leading the liturgy. Instead of asking people to stand and share their experiences, I asked them to type them into an online conferencing app. Instead of the full-bodied singing of people around me in our sanctuary, I heard the one or two voices of choir members sheltering in place. I had to rewrite prayers not only to reflect the conditions of the pandemic but also the effect of the words on people living in isolation. I had to look in new ways for the spontaneous moments of grace that happen when we pray online. I discovered that not everything I take for granted about the liturgy worked online. But I found that my desire to feel connected to my people was the same, whether online or in person. More than anything, I learned the pain and joy of loving my people.

Liturgical Lessons from the Pandemic

The core question to ask is still about the purpose of worship. The answer must always be about transformation in our lives that comes when we glorify the Triune God. We craft the liturgy so it can open our eyes to see more of God's presence in the world around us. It is this vision that restores our hope and brings us from the death of sin to the new life of grace. Our lives are transformed when we take risks in the liturgy, finding new ways to use ritual texts and actions. In the pandemic, I learned that people crave connection and will seek it any way they can. The liturgy connects us.

The liturgy is always full of surprises: someone says the wrong thing, or moves in the wrong direction, or sings the wrong notes. Sometimes we try and over-plan the liturgy to prevent mistakes, but they still happen. Mistakes are like weeds: they're just useful plants in the wrong place. When we are caught up short by mistakes in the liturgy, it is an invitation to improvisation. These are moments of grace, apertures through which to see God in a new way. When we take risks, embrace imperfections, and welcome the unexpected, we have a chance of making something new out of what we have done and said before. Just like our life in the world, the liturgy holds surprises, limitations, and promises. To find these, we have to tear up our plans and start over again. The liturgy is fearless.

Of course we can't plan on failure; we need a blueprint to show us how to build the liturgy. The Book of Common Prayer is the best guide that Episcopalians have for this work. Within it is everything that we need for common worship. This does not mean that the prayer book is perfect; it's just good enough in the meantime. The prayer book gives us instructions for how to worship, but its rites, rubrics, and guidelines are only a starting point for crafting liturgy. We must take the unique contexts in which we use the prayer book into consideration when we practice the art of disruption. We must attend to the pastoral events, cycles of nature, and rhythms of our social environment when we craft the liturgy. The liturgy is contextual.

God wants to be known in the liturgy. One of the ways we know God is by sharing our stories. People bring a universe of experiences, sensitivities, insights, and wisdom when they come to the liturgy. Everything we need is here already. Welcoming people into worship changes the way we know each other and understand prayer. Although it can be challenging to accept, change is the best gift people bring with them when they come to worship. Sometimes we will fear their gifts, but the promise of Jesus to us is that love casts out fear. The liturgy reveals God.

We can live fearlessly because Christ rose. We have to be honest about our fear. And we have to recognize that fear is never the last word. God brings life to every death that tempts us to despair, so the liturgy asks us to look for signs of the Resurrection. We have to look hard at the liturgy and find ways to highlight the Resurrection in every act of worship. We must attend to the deep desire God gives us to connect. We are built for love, to behold love in our mutual relationships and to recognize that it is in loving others that God is present with us. You may not believe in

God, but if you have ever felt love for another, you have known God. The liturgy raises the dead.

God uses everything in creation to transform us. God's revelation in beauty may be the most disruptive encounter we have in the liturgy. As we encounter beauty, it has the power to break our hearts and chase away our cynicism. Beauty is all around us, even when we do not recognize it. But our hunger for beauty is deeply ingrained in us; it approaches us as we desire it. This is why privileging beauty in the liturgy is non-negotiable; if we take it for granted, we cut people off from divine encounter. Beauty invites us to reconsider the world around us; it directs us to loving service and seeking justice. The liturgy is beautiful.

Core Values for Liturgy

I love to think about the core values of the liturgy—and I know that these values are only useful if we use them. We need these guiding lights when we decide to disrupt the liturgy and practice improvisation. If we don't name them and use them, we will make bad choices. Then we are like somebody running with a pair of scissors in their hand, causing untold damage to the church. Here is a set of core values that guide us in making liturgy at St. Gregory's.

Liturgy Is for Transformation

I witness the transformative power of the liturgy in Holy Baptism. Bradley came to St. Gregory's after being in a recovery group for a few months; his sobriety had become the central work in his life. A part of this work brought him to my office, where we would talk about the challenge of letting go to a higher power. These conversations led him to seek baptism. We baptized Bradley on a bright All Saints Sunday. Along with his presenters for baptism, a group of people from his recovery group joined us.

After I administered the water, asked the community to join him in the Covenant of Baptism, and sealed him with Chrism, I led the congregation to the altar for communion. Over and over we sang the verse, "As many as have been baptized have put on Christ." As we entered the rotunda, I looked back at where Bradley was still standing by the font, his eyes closed and facing the sun. I was overcome by the transformative power of God's Spirit that filled Bradley, the congregation, and me. I felt a little light-headed and asked someone to take my pulse. We didn't need anything other than our willingness to be transformed, and the whole community was transformed in the waters of baptism.

The liturgy calls us to new life. Transformation is hard work; it takes time, energy, and courage. The temptation is to try and bypass the hard work of transformation and make the liturgy about something else, like cheap comfort. And too often we who lead the liturgy look for techniques that will spice up the liturgy without thinking of transformation. As my friend Jimmy once said to me, "The problem is that we spend too much time looking for the killer app that will save the church." There is no killer app. There is no single way to disrupt the liturgy. What we have is the desire of God's people for a new life. The core value of transformation means that we expect the liturgy to transform people's lives.

Liturgy Welcomes Mystery

In the pandemic, we had to learn about worship with physical distancing. From a public health perspective, we were containing the spread of an epidemic. From a gospel perspective, we were loving and caring for our neighbors. Ultimately, what made that time bearable was the same thing that Jesus promised the Samaritan woman at the well: living water welling up within us. We were invited into the same mystery into which Jesus invited the woman: "The water that I will give will become in [you] a spring of water gushing up to eternal life" (John 4:14). It was not something that came from outside of her, not like the water that came up from the well. The mystery that Jesus offers us comes from the well of his life; he offers us God's indwelling Spirit.

The mystery of God's Spirit was the power that preserved us in the pandemic. In the wilderness of churches being closed and sacraments denied, the Spirit was with us. The mystery was God's love being poured into our hearts. Through the long days of isolation, God continued with us, welling up in our lives. The mystery of God's presence is always with us in our greatest need, when we were least able to help ourselves.

In that time, when the lights in the churches were out, when it felt like frightening days were ahead, when we had to keep our distance from each other, the Spirit of God continued to well up in us. That Spirit gave us the power to kindle a fire in cold hearts. God's Spirit is the wind that raises us from the dead to eternal life. Every time we logged online for another streaming liturgy, the same Spirit was with us, strengthening the bonds of love between us. The mystery of God's presence was in the love we shared in those days of physical distancing.

The heart of the liturgy is the love of God freely given to everyone. Mystery is not something that floats around us like an atmosphere—here one minute and gone the next. Instead, God's love is always with us. When we gather in the liturgy, God is present in the moment, desiring to be recognized by us. We don't have to rely on tricks to make it seem that something mysterious is happening. We don't have to lift the altar far from the people or insist on a ritual action that separates people from God. Exclusivity only results in alienation. The core value of mystery means we put your heart and trust in God's indwelling Spirit every time we come to the liturgy.

Liturgy Is Discipleship

At St. Gregory's, we place a premium on giving work away. We invite people into leadership because the work of the church is theirs. We don't spend a lot of time training people or certifying them to do their work. We're not careless in this approach. Instead, we understand participation in the liturgy to be the best training ground for leadership. Because we have a lot of people who share leadership, there's a sense that somebody has your back when you're leading worship.

Each Sunday, before the service begins, those who have a paten are supposed to ask someone to carry two chalices of wine. When we serve communion, it isn't along an altar rail; everyone is standing around the altar, and we take the bread and wine to them through the crowd, giving communion to each by name. At the end of the Great Thanksgiving, the presider sings, "Holy things for holy people," and everyone who will serve communion raises the gifts up as we sing, "One is holy, one is Lord, Jesus Christ to the glory of God our mothering Father." Just as we were about to raise the gifts, I realized that I hadn't asked anyone to take the chalices. The first person I saw was Nicholas. At that time, he'd been a eucharistic minister for eight years. Nicholas was fourteen years old at the time; he had been a communion minister since he was six. So, when I looked at him and asked him to join us at the altar, Nicholas didn't miss a beat. He stepped up, took the two chalices, and raised them in the air like it was the most natural thing in the world. Giving work away is how we practice discipleship.

Our sense of discipleship in the liturgy comes from sharing our expertise and love of the work of liturgy. This means that it isn't a crisis when something slips through the cracks, like the rector forgetting to ask someone to carry chalices; there is always someone there to help. We prepare the liturgy both for the people who always come to worship and for visitors. We welcome young people and adults to lead. We give spoken directions throughout the service, and we freely ask for help. The liturgy is where we teach what liturgy is. The core value of discipleship means that the liturgy makes people strong and resilient and able to lead.

Liturgy Is Generous

The story of my married life began in surprise. I had given up on the idea of marriage; I did not plan on falling in love. Falling in love was about the last thing I had in mind when I received a call on my cell phone: "This is Grant Martin, and I'm calling to ask you out on a date." I was sitting in the Chicago airport, waiting to return home after a three-day liturgical conference. Within a month of that phone call, I was in love. Then that sense of love began to grow, to well up in me beyond my control. It took a year before I dared to believe that love was God's call to me to become a new sort of person, one who would make a lifelong commitment to another. I love the way that the poet Jane Kenyon names the surprising experience:

> I am the one whose love
> overcomes you, already with you
> when you think to call my name . . .[1]

Even before I was ready for it to happen, even before I could think to call this new thing in my life *love*, there it was, already with me. Before I believed that it was real, love was changing me. I became who I am because I was already being shaped by love. In the same way, God's generosity is with us before we know that it is.

We sing a song with the simple words, "What we need is here." We sing the words to a melody by Amy McCreath,[2] words that come from a poem by Wendell Berry.[3] Generosity in the liturgy means that our worship is always in the context of God's loving grace. God gives us what we need to pray; the liturgy calls for our complete dependence on God as we gather to worship. God's generosity frees us to welcome everyone into the liturgy, despite our mismatched agendas, needs, longings, and doubts. We accept the gift of God's grace by generously welcoming the prepared and the unprepared, the saint and the sinner, the expert and the amateur. In this welcome, we proclaim God's universal love

1. Jane Kenyon, "Briefly It Enters, and Briefly Speaks," in *Collected Poems* (Saint Paul, MN: Graywolf Press, 2005), 137. Copyright © 2005 by The Estate of Jane Kenyon. Reprinted with the permission of The Permissions Company, LLC on behalf of Graywolf Press, *www.graywolfpress.org*.

2. Annamarie Hoos, "Paperless Songs of Abundance and Grace," Music that Makes Community, *https://www.musicthatmakescommunity.org/paperless_songs_for_abundance_and_grace*, accessed April 30, 2020.

3. Wendell Berry, "The Wild Geese," in *The Country of Marriage* (Berkeley, CA: Counterpoint, 2013).

and infinite generosity. In the ordinary course of our lives, suddenly there is God; this is the revelation of God in Jesus Christ. The core value of generosity means we plan and execute the liturgy to reflect God's grace in all we do.

Liturgy Is Guided by Affection

St. Gregory's Maundy Thursday service takes place during dinner. Everyone gathers at tables spread out in the rotunda of the church. We sing, light the evening lamps, share the eucharist, eat dinner, and wash each other's feet around the table. The first time I presided at this kind of liturgy was a few years before I came to St. Gregory's, when I was the rector of St. Andrew's in Houston. I borrowed the plan of the service from St. Gregory's. We gathered around ten or so tables, shared communion, had our dinner, and then did the foot washing. I explained how we were going to do it, telling people to remove their shoes and go around each table taking turns washing each other's feet. Then I heard laughter.

I wasn't sure who it was coming from, then I recognized the sound of the voices and looked over and saw that it was coming from two of my vestry members. They were two good old boys; one an electrician and the other an oil industry worker. As one knelt to wash the other's feet, they just burst out in laughter. At first I thought these two guys were laughing because it was just so far out of their experience. I thought there was an edge of "What is this crazy new rector making us do now?" But then I backed away from my prejudgment and looked at what was happening. It wasn't about their discomfort or doubt; they were genuinely delighting in the experience. Their laughter was a way of communicating their affection and delight.

The liturgy is a sign of God's love for the human family and all creation. This tells me that despite everything else we bring to worship, we must bring our love. Affection in the liturgy is not the same as personal affection we may have for another. Instead, it is orienting ourselves to others in service. Just as

Jesus instituted his rule of love by washing the disciples' feet, we show our love in serving others. This is the love that opens us to transcendence.

The liturgy can create a feeling of transcendence in all sorts of harmful ways—through fear, exclusion, or manipulation. But we do not have to use these kinds of things in the liturgy. When we are affectionately related to one another and God, we don't have time to be distracted by fear of the other. We always come into God's presence as beloved children, each of us equally loved by God. The meeting place of human and divine love is known by a name—Jesus. When we are affectionately related to each other, we show the real presence of Jesus in our gathering. The core value of affection means the liturgy is where we learn to value all of creation as beloved.

The Liturgy Is Popular

We make a lot of what we use in the liturgy at St. Gregory's: chalices, vestments, incense, icons, prayers, and songs. We ask the members of our congregation who have a passion for creating art to make what we need because it reflects our desire to engage in the creation of beauty. Not all of the people who create these things for the liturgy began their lives thinking that they were either artists or artists who could make sacred art.

We have a whole cohort of iconographers at St. Gregory's who gather twice a month to paint icons in the church. Our leader is a woman who just decided that she wanted to learn more about icons as a part of her life in the church and ended up becoming a painter of icons. The same goes for people who write hymns, or sew vestments, or compose texts or make chalices; they have taken up the work as a part of the joy of their life in the community. Few of us are experts at this work, and fewer still earn their living by what they make. We gather dozens of people to make the liturgy happen. We work hard, and all of it makes the community grow more robust and more real for us, strengthening us to do God's work in the world. The same feeling of camaraderie and creative engagement I've had in studio art classes is what I experience in making liturgy together.

Instead of belonging to an initiated few, preparing for worship is open to everyone. This is how the liturgy is popular: of the people. There is a liveliness to what we do in worship because it comes from the lives of those who come and pray. The celebration of the liturgy is alive not because we try to manufacture a certain feeling, but because we give ourselves over to the immediacy of the liturgy. Worship is more like a birthday dinner than it is like a trip to the theater. We don't ask people to willingly suspend their disbelief in the liturgy or hold make-believe ideas about themselves or the world around them. We ask people to come with their gifts and abilities and make church together. The core value of popular liturgy means that we invite as many people to make the liturgy as we can.

Where Are We Going Next?

When I became an Episcopalian in 1986, I assumed that the forms of worship contained in the prayer book had been around forever. Occasionally I would hear someone talk about the "old" prayer book and the "new" prayer book, but for me there was only *the* prayer book. The text of the book lifted my heart, mind, and soul to a place that I had only barely been able to imagine in my cradle denomination. You know the phrases: "Ourselves, our souls and bodies," "Will you respect the dignity of every human being," and even the slightly Star Trek sounding "vast expanse of interstellar space."

Far from being a tome dropped down from heaven, however, people like you and me write our common worship. Since joining the Standing Committee on Liturgy and Music in 2015, I have been listening to regular Episcopalians just like me, talking about a new revision of the Book of Common Prayer. We are passionate lovers of language, valiant guardians of tradition, blazing witnesses to God's loving justice, and people who hope that the way we use words in prayer has the power to transform our lives. The

Book of Common Prayer is ours to make and remake. It is ours to love enough to revise and reform and fight over and fall in love with again.

Everyone knows that one day the Episcopal Church will revise the 1979 Book of Common Prayer. It's just going to happen. It may happen in a few years or a few decades. It takes two consecutive meetings of the General Convention to authorize a prayer book. It took something like twenty-nine years to write, edit, and authorize the current prayer book. And we've been working on the revision of the Book of Common Prayer for years already. All of the "trial use" rites since the late 1980s are intended to add to the next Book of Common Prayer. We have a lot of material that people have been praying for decades. Many of these prayers are beloved and assumed by many to be a regular part of our liturgy. And that is the purpose of *trial* use: to see what sounds mellifluous to the church, what can bear the weight of our theology, and what points us to God our Creator, through Jesus our Savior, in the power of the Holy Spirit. Above all, any Book of Common Prayer must empower God's people to pray.

For more than forty years, St. Gregory of Nyssa Episcopal Church has been at work on the project of prayer book revision. We don't always admit this fact; more often than not, it feels like we're just making church together. The way we make the liturgy is simple and straightforward: we write prayers, pray them, and then rewrite them until they free us to pray with our whole hearts. We have something like twenty different eucharistic prayers that we regularly use. We have used some of these for more than forty years, and we still discover occasions to write new prayers. These prayers are by clergy and laity, poets and pastors, and people who love to craft liturgical prayer. We make them all available on our webpage and encourage people to use them in their own congregations.

Hundreds of people have come to spend time at St. Gregory's, giving us more opportunities to practice hospitality. People come to us, asking us about our practice, learning from our mistakes and successes. And we learn from these people as well.

Our experience at St. Gregory's tells me that everyone who comes through our doors is a potential collaborator in the work of prayer book revision. Seminary interns, spiritual tourists, people looking for handouts, impatient children, hungry women, outcasts from other denominations—all of these friends of God share in the work of making church. The gifts that we receive from friends and strangers are enough for us to find inspiration and courage.

The only thing that will hold us back in pursuit of transformative liturgy is fear. As my psychoanalyst told me decades ago, "Fear is the primary emotion that underlies all the others that wreck our lives." We try and hide our fear with anger, or arrogance, or insecurity, or self-hatred; at least I have. What the church needs today is the only power that casts out fear: love.

Love is the cardinal virtue that can guide each of us in the work of creating the liturgy and strengthening the community. We can love the music out of the choir and love the linens out of the altar guild. We can love the children who yell in the middle of the sermon and the unhoused visitor who weeps through the hymns. We can love the professional musician who dedicates her life to the pursuit of beauty and the amateur who can't keep a pitch. We can love all of these who share in making the liturgy because we have been brought from death to new life by the power of love that springs forth from the empty tomb.

No matter what direction liturgical revision goes, it must be in the direction of love. The liturgy is worth disrupting. Our worship deserves improvisation. And everything that comes from our work must be offered to God who loves and does not hate, and welcomes everyone to join the chorus of praise that rings through eternity. I can't wait to see what comes next.